G000079488
GRIEVING
HEART

Joyce Vixie Rigsby

AUTUMN HOUSE® PUBLISHING COMPANY
P.O. Box 1139, Hagerstown, Maryland 21741-1139

The author assumes full responsibility for the accuracy of all facts and quotations as cited in this book.

This book was
Edited by James Cavil
Designed by Bill Kirstein
Cover Photos: Comstock, INC./Michael Stuckey
Typeset: Berkeley Old Style

PRINTED IN U.S.A.

96 95 94 93 92 91   10 9 8 7 6 5 4 3 2 1

AH Cataloging Service
Rigsby, Joyce Vixie.
My grieving heart.

1. Bereavement—Self-help. I. Title.
   155.9

ISBN 1-878951-07-6

Contents

Preface

Dear Reader,

I have traveled through major tragedy, grieved effectively, and grown. Now I am starting to count my triumphs—every small one can make a big difference in my life.

Mourning for a death is a special instance of the management of loss, but its principles can be generalized. Last year my 6-year-old granddaughter Meg and I talked about how it feels to give up a parent's sole attention. How it feels to share time, toys, and space with little sisters.

We all experience daily "small deaths" accompanied by gains that can never be enjoyed to the fullest unless the losses are faced and worked through. It is only by facing and experiencing loss that we are able to face our own mortality and live life to the fullest.

Grief is never a tidy package, and all packages are different in size, shape, and contents. One author writes of the dynamics, another of the patterns, and yet another of the tasks of grief. Elisabeth Kübler-Ross's stages of death and dying is probably the best-known theory.

And the needs of you as readers are not all the same. The "heart" person may enjoy more narrative, while the "head" person may want only theory with a few illustrations. I have combined the two approaches because some heads can be reached only through the heart and some hearts can be reached only through the head. A well-integrated person is able to move at will from heart to head.

If you are grieving, I wish I could be with you in person. I would like to listen to you, touch you, or maybe just sit quietly with you. My hope is that my sharing will help you feel less alone.

If you are a comforter, I hope you will find some ways that will help you feel more comfortable with the one who is grieving.

Warmly,

Joyce Rigsby

Note: Names of support group members have been changed.

And can it be that in a world so full and busy, the loss of one weak creature makes a void in any heart so wide and deep that nothing but the width and depth of vast eternity can fill it up?

—Charles Dickens

Chapter 1

THE END

I felt a gentle touch on my shoulder and awakened instantly from a light sleep.

The room was cool, but I pushed aside the blankets that covered me. A dim light glowed in the hallway. A sliver of light from the hallway fell across the floor, across my friend Mirna's feet.

I spoke without looking up. "Bob is gone." It was as if *I* had the information, as if *I* were the one with the message that would change the rest of my life.

Mirna nodded, and I felt her arms around me. "Yes," she murmured. "At 12:30."

She switched on the bedside light in her guest room. Squinting, I finally focused on the tiny hands of my watch. Twelve forty-five.

Mirna's touch lingered on my shoulder. As she turned to leave the room, she said, "I'll keep Shirley's baby."

A few hours earlier Shirley, our eldest daughter, had arrived from California with 2-week-old Ashley. Shirley so much wanted Bob to see her new baby before he died.

When she entered the hospital room early that evening,

Bob lay motionless: his eyes were closed, and a morphine pump was attached to his right arm. In a daze Shirley crossed the room, propped Bob's left arm, and laid the strawberry-blonde baby in it. Our anguished question was Does he know she's here?

And then Ashley started to cry. Bob struggled as if to say something. A tear slid down his cheek. Was he too regretting that he would never see this baby or pick her up?

Jim, our pastor of 12 years, stood at the foot of the bed. He had shared in our joy at the weddings of our four children and the births of our five granddaughters. He also shared our pain and anguish, our alternating hope and despair, during the four and a half months since Bob's tumor had been found.

Now Jim broke the silence as he looked at the 2-week-old baby girl in the crooked arm of his dying friend: "Both ends of life so dependent on others for everything." He didn't see Bob alive again. It was December 12, five weeks before Bob's sixty-second birthday.

Early that Friday morning I fed Bob a few bites. He was too tired to chew, and when he said, "I just want to die today," I knew the time had come for me to let go. For me, "letting go" meant acknowledging on an emotional level that there was no hope left.

Ever since we had moved to our retirement dream home in early October, I had denied that Bob would die. My head knew that probably I would be left alone, but my heart refused to accept the possibility. I had avoided unmanageable distress by not allowing myself to acknowledge that he was dying.

And I knew he needed my acknowledgment that he was leaving me forever in this life. I had never imagined myself in a world without him. He had encouraged me to understand our finances, know where the well was, and how the furnace worked. I hadn't paid attention, because I hoped I wouldn't need to know. If I didn't know, he surely wouldn't leave me.

Now with surface calm and inner turmoil, I told him I loved him. I thanked him for all he had meant to me for 40 years, and told him that I would miss him—though then I had no idea of the tremendous void his death would leave in my life.

December 13, 1986, I protested Bob's death with bitter tears. Why, oh, why had such a loving, caring, and involved person been taken by death from a world that was in short supply of those qualities? It was a cry of pain and protest, not a request for a theological explanation.

I didn't know then the depths of despair to which I would plunge. I didn't know the lengths to which many in society go to avoid contact with the mourner. I didn't know the peripheral status of a single person in our society.

Nor did I know the extent to which our four children, my brother, and Bob's siblings would be there and form a safety net for me. Or how much one loving, caring, and involved neighbor could mean.

I only knew for sure that the God who was with me through the "valley of the shadow of death" would stay with me through the difficult days to come.

"Sometimes possessions, roles, and people are wrenched from us. Sometimes we choose to let go. Either way there is often a difficult adjustment and pain involved.

" 'Letting go and being let go' is a key issue in our individual growth and development. Anyone who is capable of being attached to someone also faces the risk and pain of letting go" (Ainsworth-Smith and Speck, *Letting Go*, p. 35).

Like other time-honored ceremonies, the ceremonies of leavetaking respond to profound human needs.
—Ira Glick, Robert Weiss, and Colin Parkes

Chapter 2

WRAPPED IN A QUILT

After Mirna awakened me, Shirley and I hurriedly dressed and slipped out into the cold December night. The sky was hung with stars and the windows with Christmas lights. I thought of the hundreds of times Bob had driven the same road at all hours and in all kinds of weather. Of the many times we had driven it together—and the car wheels seemed to chant "never again," "never again."

My chest felt constricted, as if bound tightly yet certain to explode if the binding were removed. I operated as at least two different people: both were sorrowful, but one was numb and detached enough to function, while the other was overwhelmed with pain, anguish, and questions. I was beginning to learn the heavy quality of emptiness. And I mourned the unfinished business and lost opportunities of our relationship.

I scolded myself for not having been with Bob when he died. The numbness of grief kept me from experiencing the full impact of my guilt until later. But even then I wondered, "Should I have left him even if it was only two miles to Mirna's house?" "Should I have left Dottie alone with Bob?"

As I think back, I realize that leaving was a part of me denying he was really dying. When daughter-in-law Dottie firmly stated, "I'm staying with Dad tonight; do you want to stay too?" I had chosen to get a little rest before what I knew would be a difficult day if he lived or died.

We all react differently in times of crises. Dottie, a nurse, needed to stay with Bob. I needed to distance myself temporarily from the intensity of the hospital room where death hovered. Death was a reality I was not prepared to meet. Now I'm sorry I didn't stay, but I did the best I could at the time. (Joyce Brothers will probably never know how much it meant to me that she also left her dying husband to see a new grandchild, and was sleeping nearby when he died.)

My foremost thought that December night was to get to Bob. We hurried through the familiar halls and took the elevator to the fourth floor. I ran to the bed and hugged his still-warm body for the last time. Never again would the telephone interrupt his sleep. (He was an obstetrician.) Never again would I feel the loving pressure of his arms around me. Never again would his lips say "I love you." Seeing Bob's body was an important first step from disbelief to belief that he was dead.

Shirley spoke first after scanning the faces of those around the bed—nurses (including Dottie), doctors, and hospital chaplain.

"I want Jim to come."

A nurse slipped out to phone our pastor, and soon he stood again at the foot of the bed and cried with us.

We all have different needs in bringing closure after a death or other separation experience. Jim needed to know the time and place of the wake and funeral so he could tell the congregation he would face in a few hours. The surgeon wanted to do an autopsy, and I signed the permission slip through tears and without adequate thought or consultation with the children.

Shirley was unable to state her need as clearly as the pastor and the surgeon. Leaving Bob's dead body too soon that night is one of her regrets. Too often we don't state our needs. We may be ashamed of them, fear the judgment of others, or simply be unaware of their importance at the time.

By Sabbath morning I could see a number of things more clearly. Of immediate concern was the autopsy permission I had signed. Bob and I had never talked about the possibility of an autopsy request. Shirley and Dottie could not bear the thought of what seemed like another assault on his body. He already had an 18-inch scar following the removal of his left kidney with a large tumor. And we knew the cancer had metastasized throughout his body.

Issues like this can split families in crises, so that instead of working together and supporting each other, they work at cross-purposes. I was sorry I'd signed but felt helpless to revoke my signature until son Bobby called just before he left Baltimore. Dottie told him our dilemma, and he simply said, "Dad and I talked about that. He didn't want an autopsy."

The solution was then simple. I risked waking the surgeon at an indecently early hour and told him I'd changed my mind about the autopsy. After all, the children had only one father. Their wishes and family unity were more important than anything else right then. The clear lines of communication between the children and me were invaluable. Each felt able to share needs and feelings, knowing they would be considered and acted on as far as humanly possible.

The predominant theme of my prayers regarding the wake and funeral was "God, please make this experience one that in years to come, when the hurt has lessened, we will remember with joy as well as sadness."

I had a model. Bob's mother had died seven months before, and the funeral was a time of sorrow and drawing closer together. It reunited those whose lives had touched hers, and provided a temporary but important support group. I knew a funeral could be a reaffirming of remaining family bonds.

But I also I knew that in our extreme vulnerability we could draw apart when we needed each other the most. On December 13, 1986, we needed each other as never before. When Bobby hung up, I phoned my daughter Marla, who was 45 miles away in South Lancaster.

"I have an appointment with the funeral director at 9:00. Can you meet me there?" I asked, and added, "Bring a suit for Daddy."

"Which one?" she questioned.

Together we decided on a jogging suit that was an early Christmas gift. I'm sure our selection surprised some, but it was right for us, and we felt Bob would have been pleased with our choice.

Then there was a long pause. Marla broke the silence.

"Do you think Shirley would mind if I wrapped Daddy in the quilt she gave us for a wedding gift?"

Shirley had designed and made a special Christmas quilt as a wedding gift to Marla and Jerry, who were married December 23, 1980.

Marla went on, "Daddy loved wrapping himself in a quilt, and that quilt is my most treasured earthly possession."

I handed the phone to Shirley. A couple hours later when Marla and I met at the funeral parlor, she had the jogging suit—and the quilt. Marla did what she needed to in order to gain some feeling of closure around Bob's death.

Shirley placed the last letter she'd written Bob in the jogging suit pocket. Fortunately it was a long one that had arrived in time for him to appreciate it. Before the wake in Stoneham on Sunday evening, each family member had some small item in Bob's pocket.

At the wake I did not try to be brave and end up with a backlog of tears. Many were strong for me. I could weep on their shoulders knowing they would accept my tears as a tribute to our friendship. I could comfort a few, and that felt right too.

Some could not look at Bob in the coffin. Maybe they didn't realize the importance of taking this first step toward accepting the reality of his death. Little Heather toddled around, and when Bobby lifted her up to see Bob she threw her pacifier into the coffin. He looked peacefully asleep, and she had shared with him during the weeks she and Dottie stayed with us before Bob died.

Monday morning, the day of the funeral, I sat in the bright sunshine that flooded our family room overlooking Lake Waushacum. It was there I had worshiped and wept, adored and railed. Our children were all home, but Bob didn't know it. The beautiful surroundings seemed to mock my pain, and my only peace came in denying that Bob was gone from this life forever. The family circle was prematurely broken.

I dressed in his favorite color—blue—and we drove the 45 miles back to our old community and church. Besides the floral tributes, candles and Christmas evergreens decorated the windowsills; poinsettias and a Christmas tree graced the platform. Though I knew that release from pain was a blessing, I found it hard to rejoice in Christ's birth at the same time I was mourning Bob's death.

Bob would have applauded the pastor's choice of the academy choir to sing special music. It was composed of students I knew and loved, as I had worked with them as guidance counselor for years. The harmony of young voices singing "Nearer, Still Nearer" was all-enveloping and comforting. Bob was "safe in the arms of Jesus."

The tributes? . . . unselfish and untiring service." "His mission in life was to show the character of his Creator to each person he touched and to reveal practical Christianity." "He exemplified Christianity." "Even in the most stressful situation he maintained a calmness—which set the atmosphere for all to perform at their best . . ."

"A prince . . . [has] fallen" (2 Sam. 3:38) is the text that stays with me. And only now do the implications of my fortune of living with a prince for 40 years flood over me. The song the choir sang at the end of the service, "When Peace, Like a River" did not reflect my feelings, but was a goal to reach toward.

On the way to the cemetery Shirley shared her version of how she felt the devil might have approached God.

" 'You know that Bob Rigsby down there has just too much going for him. Devoted wife, four loving children happily married, five beautiful granddaughters, a job he loves, with colleagues, patients, and friends who love him.'

"And the devil determined to invade Bob's body. The Lord allowed, but He laid down conditions.

" 'There must be a time for a family reunion and sharing how much they mean to each other. There must be minimal pain, and the passing must be peaceful.'

"And," she concluded, "the conditions were all met." She found the use of fantasy helpful.

Bobby summed everything up after the funeral. "It was a perfect death and funeral—20 years too soon."

We can all look back on those difficult days as a time that drew us closer together, and to God, whom we trust despite the fact that we do not understand why Bob died. We can now more fully appreciate our rich inheritance of memory and thank God for Bob's life.

"We need rituals to take us through significant emotional experiences. After death the funeral is the final saying 'Goodbye.' " Only now do I realize the full significance of Chaplain Arby Carlisle's question just before Bob's coffin was closed: "Have you said 'Goodbye'?"

"Funerals and wakes are a memorial to the dead person. We can let the community know how strongly we feel and we can support each other."

Death is the great leveler, so our writers have always told us. Of course they are right. But they have neglected to mention the uniqueness of each death—and the solitude of suffering which accompanies that uniqueness.
—*Nicholas Wolterstorff*

Chapter 3

The Uniqueness of Loss

The wake, funeral, and burial served as defenses against grief. After they were over, I came face-to-face with the daily reality of my loss and the uniqueness of my combination of losses. Patterns of loss and reactions to it are as individual as fingerprints.

I discovered, to my dismay, a network of minor losses spawned by my major loss. Any significant loss involves other losses. For example, the temporary or permanent disruption of relationships with friends is a painful aspect of reorganizing life, whether that disruption is a result of retirement, divorce, or death.

Or, after a spouse losing a job and trying unsuccessfully to find another in the same town, a family decides to move to another state, which means the other spouse must change jobs and the children change schools. This move results in relationship losses for the whole family. They may be moving away from grandparents to whom they are all close. Perhaps they will have to live in an apartment that does not allow pets, and so must give their 12-year-old dog away or have him put to sleep. A choice, yes—but also a loss.

How they handle these multiple losses that come in the wake of a job loss depends on a number of factors. Personality characteristics of each individual are important. Early losses shape our personalities and our responses to loss. Knowing how we deal with loss is important in understanding ourselves.

My parents were missionaries, and my earliest losses were those of my father. As a baby I didn't even recognize Daddy when he returned from extended trips to central Africa.

Once when I was 2, Mother and I saw him off at the train. She wept.

I asked, "Why are you crying?"

Mother answered, "Because Daddy is going away."

"But he's coming back," I reasoned.

Mother decided then that my life should not be punctuated by tears when Daddy left on trips. I don't remember seeing him off or anybody crying when he left. All I remember are joyous returns. But life is not all joyous returns to be celebrated. Life is also partings that deserve to be mourned.

There is a balance between pushing unwanted feelings out of consciousness and carrying them around on a banner for all to see every day and every hour of the day.

We all have ways by which we protect ourselves against feelings of loss. I was only 2 when I started a lifelong pattern of denying that I felt sad when Daddy left, and overemphasizing happiness at the thought of his return.

Not until I was an adult did I get in touch with the powerful emotions I felt as a child when Daddy left on trips. I now realize that I laughed at partings because it hurt too much to cry. Mark Twain said, "The secret source of humor itself is not joy but sorrow." It is possible to temporarily overcome grief and anger over loss with laughter.

Denial became one of my defenses against loss. If I

couldn't deny something, I would push it out of my consciousness—repress it. Both of these methods meant that I didn't experience the pain of loss.

Becoming aware of the ways in which my response to loss shaped my life was the beginning of the wisdom and change Judith Viorst suggests is possible in growth.

I also became aware of how repeated moves and adjustments to different communities and cultures have affected my response to loss. Frequent moving has affected my willingness to form new close attachments. Why go through the slow, often difficult process of achieving intimacy with others whom I'll eventually leave?

As an adult I prided myself on not crying when I went to the airport to see people leave. I had built my lifestyle around my 2-year-old wisdom, "Daddy is coming back." Though my wisdom increased and changed enough so that I was able to cry at the airport if I felt like it, I still had unresolved losses in my life. "Small deaths" I had never recognized, grieved over, and accepted. Systematically I went over, under, or around the pain of loss, but never chose to experience the pain. Then Bob died, and I had never really faced a significant loss.

The type of loss makes a difference in the grieving process. Each type of loss is linked with its own set of anxieties. A sudden and unexpected death that allows no preparation will sometimes almost overwhelm an individual's adaptive capacities. I remember Barb from a grief group I attended. Her husband's heart attack came entirely without warning, so the pain of her grief was compounded by shock. It also involved considerable material loss. They had bought their first new car a few months before his fatal heart attack. It was repossessed when Barb was unable to make the payments. They hadn't realized that they could have purchased insurance that would have finished paying for the car in case of death.

Another member in the grief group had nursed her husband at home for two years. When he died, the central purpose of her life was gone. And although she was worn out from long hours of nursing care, she still felt guilty to be expressing relief along with her grief. Nevertheless, this husband's death at 82 was timely, as contrasted with Barb's husband, who was in his early 50s. Women widowed in their 50s and younger oftentimes find loss and role transition very hard to handle. And the death of a child before the parent is always untimely and difficult. It alters the pattern and normal flow of life.

We had four and a half months from the diagnosis "You have a tumor on your kidney" to Bob's death. Each one of us had a chance to say the "Goodbye" that we intuitively knew would be the last. I am glad we had that time, and that Bob did not suffer more than a short while.

Suicide or homicide are forms of death that are usually unexpected and untimely. Mina from our grief group went into her garage one evening to find her husband had successfully committed suicide by hanging.

Her sorrow was compounded by shock and guilt. The day before, she had found out about his mistress and asked him to move out of their home. The path of her grief contained many setbacks. Relatives and friends blamed her for her husband's death; the only place she had the support she needed was at work.

The support, availability, and response of friends and community are important in resolving grief. I have a good friend overseas who was widowed four years ago. She manages fairly well during the day, but when the sun sets, the purposelessness of her life overwhelms her. She has no children or siblings, and there is no close person she can call or who might call her. She volunteers, but those are transient relationships with no shared history or assured continuity.

Because we had moved to a new community, I relied on my children for my sense of continuity. My phone bill was exorbitant because three of them live in California, thousands of miles away. The one consolation was that with the time difference I could phone them as late as 2:00 in the morning (they go to bed late).

Finding roles and friends in a new community takes time. Very few are capable of instant friendship. Furthermore, most are unable to deal with those in pain. It reminds them too poignantly of their own mortality. My local support system was thin but strong. A high point one day soon after Bob died was a visit to my dentist, whom we'd known for years.

Doubtless one reason widowhood hit me as hard as it did was that I had allowed myself to become too dependent on Bob. He obtained the yearly registration stickers for my car. He always pumped the gas at the self-service pump. He kept the yard up (I didn't know how to operate the lawn mower). These are little things, but they seemed overwhelming on top of other adjustments I was making.

The relationship a person has had with the deceased is a big factor in working through grief. If the relationship has been a good one with few major regrets, there will be little guilt to work through. If the relationship was poor and ended in anger and hard words, coming to terms with the loss is likely to be harder.

Another factor that makes coping with loss more difficult is other concurrent or recent losses, and previously unresolved losses. Many have never mourned the death of a parent, a miscarriage, or maybe the disappointment because a long-cherished dream will never be realized. Bob's mother died a few weeks before his cancer was diagnosed, and we had not had time to come to terms with a world without her.

Sociodemographic factors (age, sex, religion, occupation, economic position, and culture) all have their impact on the process of grieving. An occupation that takes the mind off grief while at work is helpful, but may keep the mourner too busy to grieve. An adequate financial base so the mourner does not have to work may mean too much time spent alone.

Trust that God is in control is of inestimable value during times of loss. Expecting that Christ will return does not wipe out sorrow, but does change it.

A grieving person is affected by six factors:

1. Personality characteristics.
2. Type of death or loss (sudden, unexpected).
3. Availability and response of friends.
4. Quality and type of relationship with loved one.
5. Concurrent or recent losses and unresolved losses.
6. Sociodemographic factors (economic position, age, religion, culture, occupation, sex).

One solid fact remains true for everyone. You must not walk around the perimeter of loss. Instead, you must go through the center, grief's very core, in order to continue your own life in a meaningful way.

—Carol Staudacher

Chapter 4

ALLOWING GRIEF

Colin Parkes states that grief is a process of realization, of making real inside the self an event that has already occurred in reality outside. It is the cost of commitment.

Kenneth Mitchell and Herbert Anderson define grief as "the normal but bewildering cluster of ordinary human emotions arising in response to a significant loss" (*All Our Losses, All Our Griefs*). In grief we move from one stage to another, with no definite line separating the stages. Grief softens, but never goes away completely.

Guilt, shame, loneliness, anxiety, anger, terror, bewilderment, emptiness, profound sadness, despair, helplessness: all are part of grief, and all are common to being human. Grief is the clustering of some or all of these emotions in response to loss.

In *Starting Over* Adele Nudel states, "I like the term *good grieving*. To me it means allowing oneself the full gamut of feelings during bereavement: rage, some self-pity, guilt feelings, panic, depression, despair, quiet sorrow, loneliness, hysteria, and apathy. . . . It is necessary to feel in order to heal."

At the time of Bob's death I knew myself enough to be aware of my feelings and emotions. But I would have preferred to glance at them and move on to more pleasant feelings. A lifetime of setting uncomfortable feelings aside had not prepared me for facing the pain I knew I could not avoid.

However, running away from grief and anger never prepares a person to face a loss. Successful mourners are alike in that they keep from being overwhelmed or terrorized by their loss by becoming aware of their grief and facing it.

Making the loss a reality takes the heart a lot longer than it does the head. My mind knew Bob was dead, I had seen his casket lowered into the ground, but sometimes when the phone rang I half expected he would be on the line to tell me he was coming home late because of a delivery. I spoke in terms of *we* instead of *I*. I bought too much food for one person. It was less painful to imagine Bob's presence than to accept the reality of his absence with all the strong accompanying feelings.

The day after the funeral Bob's sister helped me sort his clothes. Unconsciously I fought the reality of my loss. I cleared out only the clothes I didn't like and those that were well worn. It was as if a part of me figured he was on a long trip and would need some clothes upon return.

Bit by bit I gave the rest away, each time experiencing the pain that would bring eventual healing. Whereas I had at first been willing for Bob's clothing to occupy significant space in the closet, I finally wanted the closet empty, and came to terms with the reality that there were many empty spaces in my life besides his closet. Another might give them all away at once. In unresolved grief a room is often left as it was during the life of the deceased.

Resolving grief involves letting go of the past. The only way to go on living in a satisfying manner is to say goodbye to a relationship that is over. This also applies to people in my life who used to be close and now connect once a year at Christmas, if at all.

I must face the reality of the present and withdraw the emotional energy I invested in my relationship with Bob (and others) and reinvest that energy in new relationships. Letting go of a deep attachment, and later permitting oneself to make new attachments, are possible only when the emotions strongly associated with the loss can be felt and experienced.

A big difficulty in grieving is allowing oneself to feel and express deep feelings. Not expressing feelings is described positively in our society—"He held up well" or "She was so brave." Expressing feelings often has a negative connotation. "They broke down and wept uncontrollably."

Many take a pill, read a book, or watch TV to distract themselves from pain. Some keep busy so as not to have time to feel the pain that comes from a lack of intimate relationships. Those intolerant to pain acknowledge that a loss has occurred but insulate, isolate, and medicate themselves to avoid the pain of loss. Doctors and nurses often give powerful tranquilizers to persons in acute grief situations. These hinder healthy grieving.

Everything I read stressed the importance of expressing grief, of telling and retelling events surrounding loss and grief. I needed people, and discovered to my dismay how true is the statement that "the bereaved are isolated socially; widows in particular are ruthlessly hatcheted from invitation lists. . . . The same people who expect grieving individuals to return to work are unlikely to include them in social invitations" (Mitchell and Anderson, p. 98).

Anton Chekhov's "To Whom Shall I Tell My Grief?" became a favorite.

"It was twilight and snowing. Iona, a cabby in horse-and-buggy days, had waited since before dinner for a fare. Finally as lamplight replaced daylight, an officer seated himself in the sleigh and asked to go to Viborg. They started, and Iona looked around at the officer and with an effort said hoarsely, 'My son died this week.'

" 'Hm! What did he die of?' asked the officer.

"Iona answered, and the officer responded, 'Go on, go on, otherwise we shall not get there by tomorrow. Hurry a bit.' Several times Iona turned to look at his fare, but the latter had closed his eyes, and apparently did not want to listen.

"At Viborg Iona waited for two hours in the falling snow before he picked up three young men and started toward the Police Bridge. They laughed, joked, and urged him to hurry. He waited for a temporary silence, then turned around and murmured, 'My son—died this week.'

" 'We must all die,' sighed one of the three. 'Now hurry up.'

"Iona hurried but said, 'My son has died, and I am alive . . . death mistook the door . . . instead of coming to me, it went to my son.' He turned around to tell them how his son died, but at that moment they announced they had reached their destination.

"With an anxious and hurried look Iona searched among the crowds passing on either side of the street to find if just one person would listen to him. The crowds hurried by without noticing him or his trouble. Yet it was such an immense, illimitable grief. Should his heart break and the grief pour out, it would flow over the whole earth, it seemed. And yet no one saw it.

"Iona tried to talk to a hall porter by asking the time. 'Past nine,' he was told. 'Move on.'

"Iona moved on a few steps, doubled himself up, and

abandoned himself to his grief. He saw it as useless to turn to people for help, and started off toward the stables.

"An hour and a half later Iona told a young cab driver, '. . . but listen . . . my son is dead. Did you hear? This week in the hospital . . .' The young man hid his face and was fast asleep again.

"The old man wanted to talk. It would soon be a week since his son had died, and he had not been able to speak about it properly to anyone. He needed to tell it slowly and carefully, how his son fell ill, how he suffered, what he said before he died, and how he died. He needed to describe every detail of the funeral, and the journey to the hospital to fetch the deceased's clothes.

"Finally Iona went to look after his horse and started talking to him. 'Now let's say that you had a foal, you were that foal's mother, and suddenly, let's say, that foal went and left you to live after him. It would be sad, wouldn't it?' The little horse munched, listened, and breathed over his master's hand. . . . Iona's feelings were too much for him, and he told the little horse the whole story."

I felt a deep kinship to Chekhov's Iona. I learned how unwilling people generally are to letting themselves in for the grief, terror, and helplessness of others. Norman Paul observes, "Before a person can empathize with someone who has those feelings, he must have been able to accept their existence in himself."

In the comforting of the mourner the critical question is not "What can I say?" but "How much of this can I hear?" Most cannot tolerate another's grief enough to allow it to reecho within themselves.

Intolerance to pain is one of the obstacles to grieving. Some will acknowledge that a loss has taken place and that they are bereaved, but they cannot allow themselves to feel the pain. But unexpressed pain will slow down normal grieving, for pain then expresses itself indirectly in physical symptoms like ulcers, headaches, or arthritis.

The need to be in control of one's emotions is another hindrance to grieving. Many of us learned early to stifle expression of feelings. In families where there is an unspoken rule against the open expression of feelings, grieving is limited. (Inability to express the pain of loss is not the same as repressing the emotions of loss.)

So beside the restraints society has placed on us, we have our own need to stay in control of the situation. The fear of many is that if they start crying they will not be able to stop at will. This need to control impedes successful resolution of grief.

Chekhov's story illustrates the lack of external encouragement for the mourner to tell his story. Very few are able to really be with the sorrowing. Most want to believe the mourners are over the worst, and do their best to encourage them to look on the bright side.

Because of this inability of many to be with a mourner, the latter may be extremely isolated, and isolation intensifies grief. There are many mourners who need to have their grief heard. It is only by being heard that grief is validated.

It didn't take me many months to accept the death of the invalid Bob became. He couldn't move easily, he was in pain, and he didn't enjoy my cooking. Accepting that the healthy Bob of retirement dreams is dead is proving to be much harder. He should be here to enjoy the lake and yard. He should be here to appreciate the grandchildren's progress. He should be here to proofread what I write. The letting go is not a once-and-for-all process. It is continual. I must say goodbye to the Bob of many different roles and times in my life—to the gardener, to the listener, to the balancer, and many more.

The children in California invited me to go home with

them after the funeral. But usually part of grieving is moving back into the familiar environment once shared with the dead person. The pace is not important, and whereas one may need to spend some weeks with children before going back to an empty house, I chose to go back to the empty house and put to rest the fear that I couldn't manage there alone.

Proving that I could keep the fire going in the wood stove, that I could handle loneliness without falling apart, that I could drive up and down hills to town when the roads were icy, gave me a sense of control over my life.

Tied in with allowing my grief was gaining a new understanding of God in the face of the apparent senselessness of my loss. My confidence in God is a source of strength, but my beliefs have been challenged by Bob's death. I have grown spiritually as I have reevaluated and discovered Him as one who suffers with me.

Grief makes real the fact of loss. In order to work through grief, most mourners find it necessary to repeat the story of their loss again and again to caring friends, or sometimes to anyone who will listen. Grief is not finished at any point—it occurs again and again, usually with less intensity, each time the cycle of anniversaries, birthdays, and special days returns.

Comfort ye, comfort ye my people.

—Isaiah 40:1

Chapter 5

Comforting the Hurting

Joyfully I tore open the envelope addressed with small, precise, and familiar handwriting. A letter between Christmases—a real bonus. But a printed program announcing the memorial service of a young man fell from the envelope. My joy turned to grief. His parents were close friends from medical school days. We had lived in the same house during internship, and if I closed my eyes I could still see an adorable curly-haired toddler . . . and Bob wasn't there to share this new sorrow or edit the letter I knew I must write.

How should I contact them? I didn't even know how the boy, a man now, died. I wondered if I should phone and ask. Then I used all manner of excuses not to phone. The time zone was different. Maybe they were too broken to speak coherently. I might not be able to hear. I might not know what to say . . . My heart sank as I realized I did not know what to say despite all I'd read on the topic and even though I knew what had helped me. I phoned, and for once was relieved to be answered by a machine.

Encounters with grieving persons can be difficult. Often

the only thing they want is to restore things to the way they were before the loss, to have the dead person back. A comforter cannot do that, and the mourner cannot satisfy the comforter by seeming to be helped. So many say "I have never found it easy to say the right thing to someone who is hurting."

Saying the "right" thing is not easy, but it is infinitely more appropriate to say or do the "wrong" thing than to slip away hoping the mourner hasn't noticed your presence or won't miss your absence.

In answer to the letter I wrote, my friend responded in part, "It is hard to see folks turn and go the other way when they see us. It is like rubbing salt in a wound. If they could just say 'I'm sorry' and squeeze my hand." I sighed as I put down the letter and realized that here was another person not getting the support she needs in her grief.

Society as a whole does not handle loss, death, or grief well. Many have not been able to accept the existence of anguish, fear, and helplessness in themselves and so cannot empathize with someone who has those feelings. Most people are not able to endure the intensity of another's despair or the depth of their need. The tendency is to run away from pain, shut off complaints, or respond too quickly with clichés. But we can learn to be more effective comforters who enable hurting persons to grieve in a healthy way.

Suggesting what to say is about like telling a young person how to propose. However, there are some general guidelines that can prepare you to handle a potentially difficult interaction more comfortably.

One of the most important things you can do for the mourner is to give "respectful interest." This cannot be faked, because it comes from deep inside the listener. It is a conscious decision that the mourner is worthy of your time. It takes time. It is not asking as you pass, "How are you today?" and then rushing headlong in the opposite direction.

Merely acknowledging the loss and then changing the subject to something more comfortable for you is an affront to the mourner, who may want and need someone to listen.

Respectful interest takes into consideration the uniqueness of the hurting individual, who is affected by a number of factors. The personalities of the comforter and mourner must be kept in mind, as well as their relationship. Other considerations are the type of loss and how long ago it was, recent and concurrent losses or stresses, financial status, age, religion, and more.

If you are a close friend, you will want to phone the bereaved person immediately and stop by as soon as possible. Help acknowledge the loss. Allowing the grief-stricken to share helps to make a traumatic event real. Simply saying "I'm sorry" and waiting for a response is not enough. Be explicit. "I just heard that your mother died. I'm sorry, and want you to know I'm praying for you. Do you have a specific prayer request?" One widow wanted prayer that she would not be afraid when alone at night.

Do not seek to console by promising that things will be better, that God will take away all pain, or that time heals all wounds. They are all clichés. Hackneyed phrases like "the Lord giveth and the Lord taketh away" may only widen the gap between you and the hurting. There is no one proper thing to say, but speaking from the heart is a good guideline—though it is not wise to say everything on your heart.

You may feel that the death is a blessing, especially if the deceased was very old and in a lot of pain or severely handicapped. But the survivor may have built a life around caring for the loved one. Instead of saying "It's a blessing she's gone," tell the bereaved "I know you'll miss her" or "I remember the many times she gave me milk and cookies after school."

Say something that will allow the hurting to express their

grief normally and appropriately, because it is important that they talk about their feelings. An open-ended question such as "How do you feel about what you are facing?" is better than a question that can be answered with a yes or no.

Accept that the feelings expressed may be unrealistic and even unfair. But if they can be explored in sympathetic company, the bereaved's own sense of reality will usually be adequate. It is not up to you to point out how unrealistic and unfair the mourner is. Agree with him or her as far as possible: "Yes, what has happened to you isn't fair and does not make sense." Never be critical or judgmental.

Saying "You can always have another one" to a parent who has had a miscarriage may be realistic but it isn't helpful. It would be better to say "I know how much being a mother means to you." To say "She wasn't good enough for you" to a man who is going through a painful divorce is not as appropriate as saying "I'm sure this is a lonely time for you. I'll stay close."

Probing questions are out of place. Asking an adult child "Why did you put your father in that nursing home?" might only make the person defensive. Saying "You've made a difficult decision; how can I best support you in it?" is better.

Asking parents of a handicapped child "What will you do with her?" is probing and not helpful. Rather say, "You'll need to get away sometimes. Would you like me to baby-sit?"

Leading questions may elicit a torrent of turmoil or be met with silence. You don't have to talk to be a comfort. Sometimes the bereaved needs companionable silence to pull it all together. If the survivor expresses nothing, don't feel you must start a conversation or do something. Be willing to be there when that person may not be very good company. Your presence is the important thing. "I don't know what to say, but I want to be with you" is often enough.

Keep trying even though you won't be on target all the time, for what is offensive at one point will be comforting at another. When someone says "I don't want to talk about it," he probably doesn't mean never. Broaching the subject once and then going away hurt or relieved because the mourner isn't ready to talk will not help resolve grief. You might choose to respond, "When you are ready to talk, I'm only a phone call away."

Words are important in communication, but so is body language. Saying to a person "Come and see me any time you want to" as you back away conveys no real willingness on your part to listen. If you are willing but in a hurry, you can lay your hand on the person's arm and say "We can talk in my office this afternoon if you have time then."

I can almost hear some of you saying "I'm not a toucher" or "Some people don't want to be touched." Taking your cues from the other is essential in any relationship and invaluable in comforting the mourner. I well remember reaching over to touch an elderly lady as she was telling about her husband's recent death. She shrank away and said, "Don't touch me." Another might not be so direct.

Did I do wrong by reaching out in what was intended as a comforting gesture? *No*. I could not know that her husband's death would affect her that way. Many who are not usually considered "touching" individuals are more open to touch immediately after a loss. Often you can't predict reactions even if you know the mourner well.

Some survivors see intimacy as a responsibility—they must hug back. Or even as an assault, for they are afraid of breaking down. So if you extend a hand or touch a shoulder and the person shrinks back or stiffens, don't proceed.

And if you do touch, there is a balance between a bear hug that leaves the survivor gasping for breath and a distant posture across the room that will only accentuate isolation.

Nicholas Wolterstorff put it well: "To comfort me, you have to come close. Come sit beside me on my mourning bench."

It is significant that most of Christ's miracles involved touching the person He healed. The "laying on of hands" can have real therapeutic value and be very reassuring.

In spite of emotional cost, there must be a willingness to engage with the mourner. Crying with the newly bereaved lets that person know that it is safe to grieve. Tears can bring comfort. Helpers can show, by their willingness to show their own feelings, that they are not ashamed or rendered useless by them. Colin Parkes states that the bereaved person is often reassured when those who are nearest show that they are not afraid to allow feelings of sadness to emerge. Sorrowing with someone can make that person feel understood and not so alone.

Loss raises questions about the meaning and purpose of life. Should the newly bereaved question "Why did God permit the death?" in all likelihood it is a cry of pain and anguish and not a request for a theological or intellectual explanation. Assure grievers that God will endure doubts and questions, but don't get so bogged down talking about God that you forget the mourner. God does not need comforters to defend Him. Nor is it helpful to quote Bible verses as a way to correct or minimize feelings.

Sharing God can be helpful. But the sharing needs to come from the depth of experience, not in the form of a Bible study. The twenty-third psalm was never so meaningful to me as at the time of Bob's death. But it came from a chaplain who was walking in the shadow of death with us, not from somebody advising on the sidelines.

Mourners do not need comforters indulging in lengthy accounts of their own past loss experiences. "My father died three years ago, so I understand some of what you're experiencing now" is enough. Adding "I know how you feel" is never appropriate. Going into the details of your feelings may fulfill your own needs but not those of the mourner, whose needs come first. Do not expect sympathy for yourself. The bereaved and hurting focus on themselves.

The most important advice is BE THERE. Any number of excuses for not visiting those who hurt come to mind. You're too busy, you don't know what to say, there are others who are closer, you don't want to intrude, and furthermore, God is the Great Comforter and you're praying He will comfort the bereaved. God is willing to be the ultimate inner strength, but He wants us to help meet emotional and physical needs in times of crises. The hurting and mourning person needs someone with a face and a skin.

The hurting need someone to BE THERE during the initial period of shock and denial, when they are numb and dazed. They need help learning to acknowledge the loss. They need comfort and practical aid. They may need help making the simplest decisions. They may need to be relieved of some of their roles and obligations.

The hurting need someone to BE THERE during the grieving period, when they are adjusting to the reality of the loss. Abrupt termination of support creates its own grief, which hinders the grieving process. They need someone when they are slowly assimilating and accommodating to a big change in their lives. They need encouragement as well as comfort during this period of disorganization.

And they need someone to BE THERE over the long haul while they are reorganizing their lives. The most valued person is the one who sticks around, who helps the bereaved establish autonomy and start building a new identity instead of withdrawing from life. And maybe even gives permission to stop grieving.

To summarize:
Listen with respectful interest.
Allow the hurting to express grief.

Accept that feelings expressed may be unrealistic or unfair.

Do not console with clichés and promises.

Ask open-ended or leading questions.

Remember the importance of body language.

Share God; don't defend Him or use the Bible as a weapon.

Speak from your heart or not at all.

Take your cues from the mourner.

Agree with the mourner as far as possible.

BE THERE.

To be able to look at the awful together with another even though the other is only the author of a book makes it less awful.

—Ira Glick, Robert Weiss, and Colin Parkes

Chapter 6

I Read

Reading was a way of finding words for what was happening inside of me. I have always loved reading and found it a wonderful distractor. I read to find kindred spirits. I read to find meaning to my inner reality of guilt, depression, and unrealized expectations. Sometimes I read to take my mind away from my own pain and anxiety.

Journals and stories of others who had lost loved ones helped me know that though I was physically alone, there were many others who had survived their losses, and if they could, so could I. At a time when I had difficulty sorting out my feelings, many of the words of writers struck a responding chord in my heart.

I understood what Nicholas Wolterstorff meant when he wrote, "There is a hole in the world now. In the place where he was, there's now just nothing. . . . Only a gap remains. . . . Only a void is left. . . . An irreplaceable person is gone. . . . The world is emptier. . . . Something is over. In the deepest levels of my existence something is finished, done. My life is divided into before and after. . . . Sometimes I think happiness is over for me. . . . But I can still laugh. . . . Perhaps what's over is happiness as a fundamental tone of my existence. Now sorrow is that. Sorrow is no longer the islands but the sea" (*Lament for a Son*, pp. 46, 47).

Wolterstorff felt he had taken his 25-year-old son Eric too much for granted. That he had not treasured him enough. Eric plummeted to his death while mountain climbing. "He was a gift for 25 years. When the gift was finally snatched away, I realized how great it was. . . . How can I be thankful in his gone-ness for what he was? I find I am. But the pain of the no more outweighs the gratitude of the once was. Will it always be so? I didn't know how much I loved him till he was gone. . . . Is love like that? . . . When we gather now there's always someone missing, his absence as present as our presence, his silence as loud as our speech . . . but one always gone. When we're together, we're not all together" (*ibid.*, pp. 13, 14).

Frances Gunther wrote along the same line in *Death Be Not Proud*. "All the wonderful things in life are so simple that one is not aware of their wonder until they are beyond touch. Never have I felt the wonder and beauty and joy of life so keenly as now in my grief that Johnny is not here to enjoy them." As I looked at the ever-changing beauty of the seasons around the lake, I missed being able to share the beauty with Bob. I identified with Gunther's statement "Missing him now, I am haunted by my own shortcomings. . . . How often I wish . . ."

But Gunther could not change the past, nor could Sheldon Vanauken, who wrote when his wife, Jean, died: "The manuscript has gone to the printer." Jean was irrevocably gone, and no changes were possible in their relationship.

Vanauken's book, titled *A Severe Mercy*, started a new thought process for me. Was Bob's death a mercy? I had been willing to accept that my purpose in life might be to care for an invalid. But was allowing Bob to die instead of experiencing the role of an invalid a mercy? Would being served instead of serving have been too difficult an adjustment for him to make?

We didn't get a chance to find out—the manuscript went to the printer for me too. Bob had achieved his main goals—husband, father, doctor, and missionary in every sense of the word. It ended too soon, but the manuscript of his life and our relationship was a good one.

I soon found out that although Bob died after a short illness, there was no quick resolution of my feelings. Reading made it clear to me that I was not unique in the waves of grief I experienced for a long time. Mark Twain wrote in his autobiography, "It is one of the mysteries of our nature that a man, all unprepared, can receive a thunderstroke like that [death of a loved one] and live. There is but one reasonable explanation of it. The intellect is stunned by the shock and but gropingly gathers the meaning of the words. The power to realize their full import is mercifully wanting. The mind has a dim sense of vast loss—that is all. It will take the mind and memory months and possibly years to gather the details and thus learn and know the whole extent of the loss. A man's house burns down. The smoking wreckage represents only a ruined home that was dear through years of use and pleasant associations. By and by, as the days and weeks go on, first he misses this, then that, then the other thing. And when he casts about for it, he finds that it was in that house. Always it is an *essential*—there was but one of its kind. It cannot be replaced. It was in that house. It is irrevocably lost. He did not realize that it was an essential when he had it; he only discovers it now when he finds himself balked, hampered by its absence" (p. 323).

C. S. Lewis expressed somewhat the same feeling of being balked and hampered: "Thought after thought, feeling after feeling, action after action, had H. for their object. Now their target is gone. I keep on through habit fitting an arrow to the string; then I remember and have to lay the bow down. So many roads lead thought to H. I set out on one of them. But now there's an impassable frontier-post across it. So many roads once; now so many culs-de-sac" (*A Grief Observed,* p. 55). The old life, the jokes, the arguments, the lovemaking, the tiny, heartbreaking commonplace. . . . All that is gone" (*ibid.,* p. 28).

So much that one has become accustomed to is gone, and many other interactions change. Lewis was "aware of being an embarrassment to everyone" he met. "At work, at the club, in the street, I see people," he writes, "as they approach me, trying to make up their minds whether they'll 'say something about it' or not" (*ibid.,* p. 10). Had I read that before Bob's death, I would have said to myself, "C. S. Lewis must be paranoid." Now I know he was not.

What I appreciated most about Lewis was the movement in his process. He first regarded life as a series of dead ends and later could say, "Bereavement is a universal and integral part of our experience of love. . . . It is not . . . the interruption of the dance, but the next figure" (*ibid.,* p. 59). I read that at a time that I regarded Bob's death as an interruption beyond which I could not envision a meaningful future.

I felt more atune with Lewis's observation that feeling better brought a sense of betrayal. I too felt "that one is under a sort of obligation to cherish and foment and prolong one's unhappiness" (*ibid.,* p. 62). It seemed the only way to lessen the guilt I felt because I was alive to enjoy everything Bob could not. But as Lewis progressed, he found the less he mourned H. the nearer he seemed to her. I looked forward to that time.

And to experience for myself the truth of the discovery Lily Pincus made after her husband's death, "that here too the full acceptance of the finality of the loss and all the pain that goes with it need not diminish life but could give it a new quality of fulfillment" (*Death in the Family*).

For me that meant searching for fulfillment outside instead of within the home. I could not use the same yardstick for fulfillment I had used most of my life. And I did not have to judge fulfillment outside the home as better or worse than within—only as different.

At a time that I could see no gain in death I read *Necessary Losses*, by Judith Viorst. She states that "many students of mourning maintain that in any kind of death 'there is no loss that cannot lead to gain' " (p. 263). Most would gladly forgo the gain if they could forgo the loss, but life doesn't offer us the choice.

Rabbi Harold Kushner did not have the choice when he learned that his first child, Aaron, had progeria, a rare disease producing rapid aging. Aaron would never look like the children his age and would die in his teens looking like a little old man.

Kushner writes about the question of losses and gain in *When Bad Things Happen to Good People*. "I am a more sensitive person, a more effective pastor, a more sympathetic counselor because of Aaron's life and death than I would ever have been without it. And I would give up all of those gains in a second if I could have my son back. If I could choose, I would forgo all the spiritual growth and depth that has come my way because of our experiences, and be what I was 15 years ago, an average rabbi, an indifferent counselor, helping some people and unable to help others, and the father of a bright, happy boy. But I cannot choose" (pp. 133, 134). Nor could I.

An Eastern woman whose son had died went to Buddha and said, "O Exalted One, give me medicine for my son." The

Buddha answered, "Go back to your village and find tiny grains of mustard seed from a house in which no one has died."

The woman found that every home in the village had lost someone to death. She was not alone.

Reading helped me realize I was not alone.

The author has done something I believed impossible—assuaged his own grief by conveying it.
—Anna Fremanete, of C. S. Lewis

Chapter 7

I WROTE

During the bittersweet days before Bob's death and the bitter, bitter days after his death, I wrote. I didn't want to keep my emotions bottled up, and when there wasn't a listening ear available, I wrote to my journal, Bob, and God. The sentences were often incomplete and incoherent, but I wrote, knowing the act of writing was more important than what I wrote.

November 13, 1986

I'm becoming more and more sympathetic to a young child's need of a blanket for comfort and the panic felt when the blanket is unavailable. This journal is my security blanket.

November 14

We just finished reading Bernie Siegel's *Love, Medicine, and Miracles*. I asked Bob how he visualized his tumors. "As snowballs," he answered. "And the treatment?" I questioned. "Sunlight" was his response as he lay in the sun of our family room.

November 16

Bob stayed up late to watch a large log he'd put into the fire die down. During the night I thought how the log in its burning gave pleasure and warmth to all around. And how in its dying a fire is comfortable to be near.

November 17

Each visitor has his/her own problems. They're all in need of healing to a greater or lesser degree. . . . I realize why some don't visit. They can't come without entering into our pain, and their load is already heavy.

November 20

How long will I have him? . . . I can't live with as much fear as I'm experiencing. . . . God promised, "Fear thou not; for I am with thee" (Isa. 41:10).

November 21

I feel like a pressure cooker inside. Wish I felt as calm as the lake. . . . I was surprised to get a note from Eve. . . . Let me never forget how much a few words can mean. Only 15, but they were the right ones.

November 23

This morning Bob asked, "Did you start a To Do list?" . . . It's hard for him to sit and see so much he'd like to do and not have the energy for much more than basic needs. . . . Tonight he fell at the bottom of the stairs. His left leg is too weak to hold his weight when he's tired. . . . It's painful to watch him go upstairs one step at a time, placing weight on the right foot and dragging the left.

November 26

Shirley called from California late last night. "Ashley is

on her way." Bob stayed up all night to labor with them. She is truly a Thanksgiving baby born the day before.

November 27

I've started waking up with tears in my eyes and an enormous pressure in my chest. The lake is as placid as ever—assurance that life will go on despite hurt and heartache. But the very beauty of nature brings new tears. . . . Beauty is meant to be shared. I'm not sure I have the inner strength to grow from the experience. . . . I'm angry that the retirement we've looked forward to is being denied us . . .

November 28

My problems loom like a large black cloud on a horizon that looks ever nearer. There seems no way to escape the coming storm. If I come out alone, will I be a better person because of the experience?

November 29

"Lord, for tomorrow and its needs I do not pray.
Keep me, guide me, love me, Lord, just for today."

Baby Heather leaves tomorrow. The gift of watching her develop this past month has been such a blessing. I agree with the Chinese proverb that says "One joy can scatter much pain."

November 30

What's most important to do when your days left together are numbered? . . . Last night I felt filled to the brim with liquid pain. . . . I lay beside Bob, my whole body shaking with sobs. He patted my head with a familiar and comforting gesture. How much longer will he have the strength for even that? . . . Joy and thankfulness come with the pain. Some never experience the joy of being the center of someone's life. No one can take that memory from me.

December 2

Today I took Bob to the hospital for a bone scan. I imagine the Lord asking me, "Do you want Bob spared like this?" I'm sure God's storehouse has enough strength for that, too.

December 3

They're keeping him because of high blood sugar. I decided to go to California to see Ashley while Bob is hospitalized. It was one of the hardest decisions of my life. Bob said to his physician, "I want Joyce to go so badly I can taste it." . . . Some were vocal in their disapproval. I do think the advice to "support people who have made difficult decisions" is good . . .

December 4

I saw a couple embracing at the airport and realize that Bob will probably never see me off or meet me again.

December 5

Ashley is a lovely baby—round little face, strawberry-blonde hair, chin that looks like an afterthought. . . . Bob will start radiation today. . . . Die? The word haunts me. It feels like a thief is trying to take away what I treasure most. . . . We have shared the exhilaration of world travel—New York to Tokyo, Amsterdam to Manila. At the rate things are going, a return trip from bed to bath is a major undertaking.

December 6

Bobby called saying the doctor suggested I return on Monday. . . . As I look at 10-day-old Ashley, the seed of certainty grows in me that Bob will never see her. I wonder if he'll be able to appreciate the dozens of pictures and video of her I'll be taking back. . . . Have I charged my exhausted emotional batteries? I do not want to become emotionally dead, though it would be infinitely less painful. I want to go on feeling and trying to understand.

December 8

I am on the plane home. A now-familiar pain engulfs me. I relax, close my eyes, and let the tears fall. The pain will pass if I just go with it and not fight it . . .

December 9

Bob loved the pictures and video. "It's almost as good as being there," he said as granddaughter Kaiti practically jumped out of the video into his arms. . . . But it looks like Bob's work on earth is done. What about the biblical threescore years and ten? I feel cheated. . . . Christ's work on earth was completed in 33 years, so who am I to beat the gates of heaven with my supplications and demands? . . . It's hard not to act as consultant to God, telling Him what I think He ought to do. . . . How will I manage alone without Bob? . . . Staying connected now so he won't sense withdrawal on my part and yet tying off enough so that when he dies I won't bleed to death psychologically is a difficult balance.

December 11

Speech is almost beyond me—tears are my best language now. I went to my support system at Greater Boston Academy. We cried, joined hands, and prayed. I hope God heard—I didn't. . . . We're making arrangements to take Bob home to die—Marla suggested 4-year-old Jennifer take the night shift, as she doesn't sleep anyway.

December 12

"It's harder just being with than doing for," a chaplain friend said after repeating the twenty-third psalm. . . . If I can only trust. . . . Trying to understand takes away so much energy I need for other things. . . . Someone said, "What doctor will pray with the patients if Bob dies?" . . . I wonder,

"Who will pray with me?" . . . Writing is my only sanity, though I'm down to a pencil stub. . . . Dottie and Heather arrived. . . . Bob's breathing is labored. He responds to no one. . . . His hands are cold. . . . I think back to the thrill the first time I held his hand.

December 13

He's gone. . . . I'm numb, sad, and lonely as I rock 2-week-old Ashley . . .

December 14

I never imagined myself as the widow of the deceased. . . . I torture myself by going over the past few days and thinking of what I would do differently if I could do it over. . . . I walk the house to find someone to cry with. . . . Everyone is asleep. I wonder if the babies were up in the night. . . . The trees are silhouetted against the dawn sky . . . the twinkling lights across the lake fade into daylight . . . I think of children and siblings on their way to the funeral . . .

December 15

The longest, saddest day of my life is ending. . . . I'm so tired I can hardly function, but it is almost as if by not going to bed and to sleep that I'm hanging on to a part of Bob. . . . Others reach out—always well-meaning—sometimes clumsy and tentative. Our culture does not relate well to death.

December 16

The lake is partially frozen . . . the trees and houses are not reflected as they were in the water. On the spiritual side: How can we reflect Christ if we are frozen and icy, solid and inflexible?

December 17

The full impact of these past events is mercifully wanting. It is as if my mind put the events on hold because it can take no more. . . . The magnitude of my loss is overwhelming . . . yet my grief is not obvious to most, or if obvious, they choose to ignore it. But I will express my grief in whatever way seems most appropriate at any given moment. I will not have a grief impaction within me . . .

December 18

Inconsistent and unexplainable are the ways of the mourner . . . some insignificant happening can cause tears to flow unbidden and unstoppable, while at other times I stand dry-eyed when I expect abundant tears.

December 19

Eve was all business on the phone. She offered no word of comfort. Maybe she too doesn't know how to handle death. . . . I realize that when hurtful things happen to me from now on, I have no one to share them with. . . . I do try to focus on the support I'm getting and not on what feels like indifference. . . . Teddy even canceled his patients the day of the funeral. . . . I'm having a hard time hanging on to the thought that I've been so lucky to have Bob nearly 40 years. . . . Why didn't I make a tape of Bob's voice before he died? I want to hear him say "I'm a lucky duck." We both felt so fortunate to have each other.

December 20

The Nelson boys and their wives invited us for supper (me, Marla, and family). They didn't offer words, but were just there with food, presence, and attentive ears. . . . Bob's spirit and benediction rest over this house, the lake, and my life. . . . I look at the sky and think of the hymn "The Golden Morning Is Fast Approaching."

December 21

I feel so hampered—I am not a whole person anymore . . . but I want to make this house of our dreams all that we dreamed together it would be. . . . But before that can happen, I need to tell of the recent events over and over. I cannot put them casually aside because the funeral is over and Bob is in the grave.

December 23

I'm torn between the desire to stay in the home of our dreams and the difficulties attendant to staying.

December 24

Part of me wants to live among my memories, for that is where Bob is, but memories cannot satisfy my soul hunger any more than a picture of food can satisfy a hungry man. . . . Learning to live with the pain of loss is part of the price I will pay for keeping his memory alive. I wrote on the flyleaf of a book I gave him the first Christmas we were married:

Life's greatest gift will ever be
To have your love and you.

How could I have known with such certainty back then who would bring me so much happiness? Now the bigger question is "How will I exist without life's greatest gift to me?"

Yesterday Marla and I mailed in the application for Bob's life insurance policy. It feels so crass, like trading his life for money. . . . I don't want the money, I just want him back. I know that full acceptance of my loss need not diminish my life, but can give it a new quality of fulfillment. But how do I get from here to there? . . . Music, meant to be joyous, filled the supermarket. "The Twelve Days of Christmas" is on the bottom of my list of nonfavorites. Bob died 12 days before Christmas.

December 25

How can emptiness feel so heavy? Christmas seems a charade. The gifts a mockery. I want to cut December out of the calendar forever. . . . I dread the thought of all the children going back to their homes after Christmas. They have invited me to go with them, yet I feel I have an enormous task ahead that I must do here alone. . . . I don't want grief to take the place Bob had in my life . . . I want the memories without the almost-constant pain that now attends them. . . . Christ said, "Blessed are they that mourn, for they shall be comforted" (Matt. 5:4). Will the comfort come to me, or do I have to go find comfort? . . . In view of my own total feelings of loss I must remember that the children have suffered an incalculable loss too. . . . Only Heather and Ashley go on the same as before.

December 26

I now know that when the family is together I will miss Bob the most. . . . I want to bury myself in some hole and die . . . without Bob everything seems pointless. . . . I remember being caught in the ocean undertow off an Accra beach years ago. I was powerless to get back to shore.

Grief feels like that undertow. I'm not sure how far out it will pull me, but I know I'm in water too deep for me to navigate alone. I know You're there, God, but it doesn't feel like Your arms are around me—rather that You're watching, cold and distant, to see what I'll do next . . .

December 28

Somewhere in my soul is a plot of calm surrounded by raging storm, uncertainties, doubts, and questions. I am thankful for the calm; I will focus on it. . . . Jesus of the New Testament commanded the waves to be still, and He can now.

December 30

Guide me, Lord, to something that's right for me to do. May I remember to reach out and not expect people to know what I need automatically.

January 2, 1987

A heavy snowfall blanketed the bare ground and decorated the trees. . . . There's a part of me that wants to be buried in this snow. . . . Every day is a gift, but sometimes I don't want the gift . . . . I must start measuring time in shorter increments. I must stay in the present—I can't handle past guilts or tomorrow's worries as well.

January 3

Shirley and I talked a long time on the phone about what constitutes a good death. A friend in California said Bob's was as near perfect as possible. . . . He was at peace with God and man; there were affirming friends and family, with no unfinished business to attend to at the deathbed; and his body had not withered away beyond recognition. . . . He looked natural in the coffin.

January 4

Bob died three weeks ago. I went to a new church alone for the first time. . . . I sat alone. . . . I left alone, wanting others to reach out to me . . . yet afraid that I'd cry if they did. . . . I feel like a puppet and puppeteer . . . I pull the right strings to give the illusion I'm managing. I don't break down in the wrong places—usually. I keep eating—too much. I go shopping . . . but I feel the outer shell is so thin and brittle it could break through at any time, revealing my emptiness and nothingness to everybody. . . . I'm warm, fed, and watered. . . . And if I share how overwhelmed I am at the thought of living alone, people are quick to recite how much I have going for me . . .

January 5

People who don't live up to my expectations are a target for the anger I experience relative to Bob's death. . . . I shall be happier if I quit expecting anything from anyone. Then I shall be surprised and gratified if I get it and not hurt and disappointed because it is not available. . . .

Yesterday I received four unexpected long-distance calls. All were nourishing and affirming. I struggle to think through the common thread. . . . They bypassed chitchat; they did not tell me to count my blessings; they did not scold me for my expressed anger. They let me carry the conversation . . . without imposing their agenda . . .

One author writes of the "toll this charade of sanity takes." I know what she means . . .

A clerk asked if they'd given a copy of an order. "I don't know," I answered. "My husband died since then." . . . How long will I grasp any opportunity to suck some unsuspecting passerby into my grief with me? My need is so great I forget others want to be *apart* and not *a part* of it. . . . I decided to cook cream of wheat, Bob's favorite. I gagged my way through a lumpy serving salted with tears.

January 7

My friend Dessa graciously invited me to spend last night with her family. I'm not ready to cope with the "we" of them when I'm so acutely aware of the "I-ness" of me. I spent two hours with her. We talked, cried, ate, and laughed. I felt renewed. . . .

I stopped at Marla's on the way home. She is amazed that so soon after Bob's death it's been relegated to distant past history by most. . . . On a lighter note, Jennifer just informed me, "You know, cats don't have to get married or go to the hospital to have babies. That's right."

January 9

I'm getting used to carrying my hurt without the constant need of a paper psychiatrist, my journal. . . . There were so many joys along the way in the process of learning to become a wife and later mother. Are there any joys along the path to widowhood? The joy, to be differentiated from happiness, will come as I become a person independent of others for an identity. . . .

I wept this morning as I stepped out on the ice alone. It was such a symbolic step. . . . Later I returned, joyful, to the house, grateful for a space of my own. And an acceptance that the joy and gratefulness will be tinged with pain and sorrow.

January 14

A month ago yesterday Bob died. . . . I picked up the mail, which included a check for his life insurance—a piece of paper in place of him. Slowly I drove to the bank. . . . I sat down in the bank manager's office and burst into tears. Throwing the check on her desk, I sobbed, "I don't want it. I just want Bob." At least I had the presence of mind to throw it at the right person. . . . Stopping to see Jennifer on my way to Boston was a happy interlude. "Gran is so sad—she needs a hug" brought her straight into my arms. And how she can hug!

So went the months before and after Bob's death. The following spring, while visiting friends in Texas, I met Larry Yeagley, chaplain at Huguley Memorial Hospital. "Write the history of your relationship with Bob. Start at his death and work backwards," he suggested. Tears filled my eyes, and I shook my head. "Try it from the beginning then."

Larry went on: "Tell about the first time you met him." *Easy,* I thought as I recalled the cafeteria at old Emmanuel Missionary College, where I met Bob one Sabbath dinner early in a second semester. I had just arrived from Africa, and he claimed till his death it was my South African accent that first attracted him to me.

Larry continued: "You can think 30 years in three minutes, but it takes longer to write it. That's why I suggest that grieving people keep a journal during their grief. Write down all the details, but also the feelings you have. Tell your journal how life is different without Bob. Tell about the things that help and the things that hurt. Express your anger, your loneliness, and your frustration. Be very open with your journal. This slows down your thinking and tends to lessen the pain that accompanied your first thoughts."

Yeagley's eldest son was killed in a car accident, and because Larry had traveled the path of loss and pain, I was willing to follow his suggestions. I wrote at all hours of the day and night, and writing became my favorite way of discharging emotions. I could do it anytime.

The use of metaphor in writing proved especially helpful. For example, much literature uses the seasons to describe the recovery cycles of grief.

The winter of early grief is a vision of a world without meaning. Nature is indifferent to our sorrow, and the beauty of a spring the dead one is not here to enjoy is more insult than promise.

I had a good model in the seasonal use of metaphor that started with a widow, Mary Jane Moffat, reading a small quote and expanding, moving and growing through the seasons until she had worked through her own grief and published her anthology of literature on mourning, *In the Midst of Winter*.

"Metaphorically, spring is the period of great despair and yearning, the phase of searching for that lost aspect of ourselves the dead represent. It is this pull between the future and the past that places the mourner in such a precarious position. As Lady Ise, a ninth-century Japanese poet, says, 'there is nothing left to cling to.' The work of this season of mourning is to incorporate what is precious in the past and in our memory of the dead person into our living selves. When this is accomplished, we allow ourselves to be pulled with the seasons into a summer of acceptance, where nature is imbued with meaning because we understand both heartbreak and renewal. It is then that survivors are prepared for an autumn in which we are able to view with equanimity the prospect of our own death."

Many metaphors came to mind that never got beyond the thought stage. Life was and is like a number of puzzles that have been mixed up. There are thousands of pieces. Every time I find a piece that fits into that day's puzzle I rejoice. Sometimes it seems that pieces I possess do not belong to any of my puzzles, and I wonder if I've borrowed from another's life puzzle. And some pieces are missing.

Living on a lake made the metaphor of boats and water especially applicable. My journal often alludes to this. I used to think of myself as a damaged vessel. My compass was lost, and I could not bail fast enough to keep the water out. (This became literally true when the lake rose one early spring to nearly two feet in my basement. Bailing out was impossible, as I would have had to bail the lake out. I just had to wait until the waters went down.)

In my metaphor some vessels passed and didn't see me. Some saw me but then ignored me. Others provided encouragement from a distance. A special few came close enough to be of real help. As time went on, I found that I could guide my course by the stars and that I could keep a damaged vessel afloat. And finally I acknowledged that the vessel would never be the same again and mourned the vessel that was and made appropriate changes.

The metaphor of a broken leg was helpful. Years ago we were on vacation with our four children on Spain's Costa del Sol. Affordable only because we traveled "space available" for a fraction of the usual cost. While crossing a street, we failed to notice a motorcycle. It hit Marla's leg, and she was pitched 100 feet down the road. She landed as limp as cooked spaghetti, and for eternal seconds we thought she must be dead.

Bob set her leg while she was unconscious, and we immediately took her to a small emergency hospital nearby, where a cast was applied. If I likened the cast to my support system after Bob's death, I would say it was removed too soon. Though healing takes place from within, it takes a long time and needs outer support until strong. I ask myself if I might have become so comfortable with a cast that I would never have chosen to remove it.

Likening support to crutches was more helpful. I did not need them all the time, and they were available in the form of therapist, chaplain, a few close friends, and children.

I compared my relationship losses to flat tires. Some occurred as a tire blowout—completely unexpected and causing resultant damage to the vehicle of my life. Others were like a slow leak—the loss was hardly noticeable at first, but soon interactions became farther and farther apart and had less and less substance, till the tire of my relationship with that person was completely flat. Could the tire be patched and pumped up again? Only if both the friend and I wanted that to happen. Neither could do it alone.

Writing this is forcing me to reevaluate the status of different relationships, and my daughter editor-in-residence has pointed out that Bob was the first and most important domino to fall and that other losses were the result of this domino effect.

The most effective metaphor occurred to me about nine months after Bob died. I hit an all-time low. I had expected to feel depressed in December around the anniversary of Bob's death, but not in September. Then suddenly I understood. I'd lived with an obstetrician for nearly 40 years, and his work was based on nine-month periods. This started a new line of thought. What happens after nine months? The baby is delivered. What could I deliver? Grief.

Delivering Grief did not mean I was through with it, but that I could leave it at home when I went to work. I could nurse it at home, but Grief and I didn't have to be in the same place all the time. I could look upon Grief as being outside of me. This is called disidentification.

Before the first anniversary of Bob's death I realized that though it would be a difficult time, it could be a turning point. This would be more likely to happen if I made it one. I drove to Boston and attended the first memorial service since Bob's death. In an effort to get some doubts and questions answered, I talked to the surgeon who operated on Bob. I visited the church where Bob's funeral service was held.

On the Sabbath anniversary of Bob's death I awakened early and dialogued with Grief in my journal.

Joyce: "You've been living with me now for a year. I'm afraid if you stay longer everyone will think it's a permanent arrangement."

Grief: "I call that ingratitude. I've spent a year with you keeping you company, devoting all my time and energy to you. And now you ask me to leave."

Joyce: "You have performed your function in my life. For a while you did take Bob's place, but I don't want to become a professional mourner."

Grief: "How you've changed. I remember when you wouldn't even leave the house without me. I hate to leave you alone."

Joyce: "I won't be alone for long. I'm planning to invite Hope and her children to live with me. I've been listening to her singing outside the door. I'm afraid I won't have room any longer for you and your children: Anger, Guilt, Depression, and Jealousy."

The next morning I awakened early again and dialogued with Hope.

Joyce: "I've been wondering, Hope, which of your children will be moving in with you."

Hope: "Joy, Excitement, and Peace all want to come. You knew them well before Bob's death. And then there's Expectation—"

Joyce: "I do not have room for her. She has caused me enough trouble with her visits. When she came she brought out the worst in Depression."

Hope: "What do you mean?"

Joyce: "Expectation felt people should be more supportive, and Depression threw tantrums after her visits."

Hope: "I can make other arrangements for Expectation. But did you know that Joy was married to Sorrow?"

Joyce: "Sorrow has been living here for a long time now. I had a hunch he and Joy were in a committed relationship, for it seems that the deeper my sorrow, the more joy I'm able to contain."

Hope: "I'm looking forward to living with you as you move on with your life."

I dialogued with Guilt and Anger as well. Separating out the different troublesome parts of myself and addressing them one by one was more productive than handling them all at once. Like children, my emotions were more manageable on a one-to-one basis.

Writing demands a slowed-down thinking process. It demands a clarity that is not always present in thinking. I found it a powerful tool in working through my grief. I could see where I had progressed and where I was stuck in a rut as I read what I wrote.

Give sorrow words. The grief that does not speak whispers in the o'erfraught heart and bids it break.
—William Shakespeare

Chapter 8

STRATEGIES FOR COPING WITH LOSS

Every tree around the lake was dressed for spring in delicate finery. The ice had melted, and a few motorboats were braving the chilly water. A friend's horse foaled. Babies born during the winter were taking their first stroller rides. Though I had much for which I could be thankful, I felt out of tune with the world.

Then one day Larry Lewis, head of Atlantic Union College's Psychology Department, asked me, "What would you like to do?"

"Teach a class on strategies for coping with loss," I answered, and added, "Many ways of coping apply to all losses, not just those caused by death."

Planning for that class was a giant step forward. It meant I had some structure to use the pain of grief productively. I could share my insights from the long, lonely months of reading. The class would be a place where talking about loss was expected.

I didn't know if the topic would generate enough interest to attract a class in the first place. I wondered if I'd be able to share my deep feelings without breaking down. Would it matter to the class if I cried? Would my recent hearing loss prove too great an obstacle? Planning for the class was a lifeline, and teaching it became an anchor. The class became an instant community for me. Some of the foreign students were struggling for an identity in a new country and culture, with few continuities in their lives. I knew on a day-to-day basis what it feels like to lack identity and continuity.

Some of the students had buried their feelings and not allowed themselves to experience grief after the death of a parent or grandparent. More than one shared the sense of exclusion they had experienced when, as small children, they were not permitted to go to a wake. One adolescent was not even told the time and place his dearly loved grandfather's memorial service would be.

Though the loss from death differs from losses from miscarriage, rape, or retirement, those experiencing the losses usually go through Elisabeth Kübler-Ross's grief stages of denial, anger, bargaining, depression, and finally acceptance. The order is not always the same, the cycle is repetitive, and anger is sometimes labeled "hurt." The students found that this framework on which to pin feelings surrounding loss helped them understand it better.

Because awareness of how we handle our losses is an important step in coping with them, my first assignment was to ask the students to simulate a physical loss for 24 hours. They "lost" sight, hearing, full motion in arms or legs. One fasted. As they shared how these losses felt, they became aware of how differently people react to loss.

Each one learned how to be with others in loss, how to really listen. They shared deep feelings relating to their own past and present losses. They became the kind of people everyone who experiences loss needs. And we all experience loss.

Teaching the class was one way I coped with loss that few would choose. Basically it provided a setting where talking about it was appropriate.

Many communities have support groups available for those working through losses. There are groups for widows, incest victims, and drug addicts (they have all lost control). Compassionate Friends was formed for those who have lost a child, and some hospitals have groups for parents who have gone through miscarriage. I even found a news clipping advertising a group for those who mourn pets that have died.

A group usually meets only once a week. What about the rest of the time? The too-busy days or empty days and nights when going on seems impossible? When fear and anxiety regarding the future, and guilt and anger of the past, overwhelm? When there isn't the mental or emotional space for the joy of the present?

During the days before Bob's death I'd discovered living in the now is possible. I learned then not to take on all the worries and anxieties of tomorrow or guilts of many yesterdays.

I could cut life into smaller, manageable segments. I could live each moment of the day and enjoy the beauty all around. I could experience life a bite at a time and not try to eat the whole loaf at one sitting. Living in the now became an important strategy in coping with loss.

Later as I read *The Precious Present,* by Spencer Johnson, I realized how many precious moments I had lost because I was trapped by past guilt and "if onlys," as well as anxiety about the future and "what ifs."

One Step at a Time, the inspiring story by Elena J. Hanuse of her walk across America, tells how she followed her dream from sea to shining sea. I could also take one step at a time.

This does not mean I don't plan for the future. I know I am better off if I plan to spend parts of weekends with others. Not making plans in the hope that others will include me in theirs doesn't work. Waiting to see what I feel like doing doesn't work either.

For a while Saturday evenings were the hardest. Watching TV alone held no attraction for me. I especially disliked going somewhere and arriving home alone after dark. Sometimes I would be brave on the ride home, and as soon as I'd locked the door behind me I would beat my fists against it. Though I realized discharging my feelings was better than holding them in, I decided to try planning ahead. To know that I have something to look forward to is like insurance.

The insurance takes many forms—a long-distance phone call, a special book to read, writing letters to friends are options. Now that I have a computer I am never at a loss for something fascinating to do. It even talks back to me.

Sometimes I invite a friend over for supper on Friday evening and we talk by the fire. Planned potluck groups provide for some of my need to be with other people. During the summer, friends stop by to swim, boat, and sun.

All of these activities involve planning ahead and prove rewarding as long as I don't get caught up in thinking how I need Bob here as host before I can enjoy people. I try to remember that other single people entertain successfully.

Planning ahead sometimes involves making arrangements to visit friends and children weeks or months before I intend to go. That way I get maximum benefit out of anticipating the visit. Three of my children live in warm places, and I can look forward to getting away from an extended New England winter. Even when Bob was alive I usually started planning the next trip as soon as or before one was completed. At first making trips Bob should have been along on was difficult, but gradually it became easier.

Trips aren't always to distant places. If a difficult anniversary is coming up, I may plan an overnight trip 45 miles away in Boston. Staying with friends assures me that I won't be alone with my thoughts at a difficult time.

I know that the trip home from the airport after children have visited is especially difficult. Seeing I was "born to shop," I decided after Bobby's last visit to go to a favorite discount store on the way home. I bought a sweater on sale. This eased me back into aloneness and solitude.

You might choose to sew a garment, chop wood, or paint a picture. Another might go to a library or visit with a friend.

As a last resort, there's always eating. I must limit this method of caring for myself, or my weight gain will announce to the world that overeating is my preferred method of coping with loss.

I try to time the eating, shopping, or whatever treat so as to achieve maximum emotional satisfaction. Eating a dessert at a potluck where I'm surrounded by friends doesn't give me as great an emotional lift as eating a dessert when I'm alone on a Saturday night.

I came to realize that loneliness and fatigue were a poor combination. I learned that when I wasn't too tired I had the mental and physical energy to make plans and carry them out.

But grief makes me tense. Grief makes me uptight. Grief ties me into knots. I fall asleep, but awaken soon thereafter as on edge as if I'd been handling a major crisis at work. I spend enough time in bed, but not enough time relaxing.

I need to practice relaxing at will. Years ago I learned how to breathe out worry and tension and breathe in calm and peace. I learned how to visualize myself in restful surroundings. I learned how to relax muscle groups successively. I know through experience that relaxation reduces headaches. Why not other aches?

A brisk walk or swim is a good remedy for tension.

Raking leaves or shoveling snow has the added advantage of making me feel good about the active role I am taking in keeping my yard up.

Doing yardwork is a new tradition of necessity. I prefer the ones that are choices. Mirna said during an Easter weekend visit, “Let’s make this a tradition.” I need some new traditions in my life that aren’t reminders of what Bob and I did together. A friend and I always pick strawberries at least once during camp meeting. I’m looking forward to picking again this year. Establishing traditions is one way of gaining control of my life. Choosing small challenges, reasonable and varied, that are not likely to overwhelm me is a way of exerting control over events.

Though many, possibly most, losses are beyond our control, we can choose our attitude toward those losses.

God helping me, I will choose to think creatively and to grow so I can add to my strategies for coping with loss. The possibilities are endless.

Communication is the lifeline to survival.
Avoid guilt and anxiety trips.
Live in the now.
Take one step at a time.
Plan ahead.
Practice relaxation techniques.
Reassert a degree of control over your destiny.

The greatest discovery of my generation is that human beings can alter their lives by altering their attitudes of mind.

—*William James*

Chapter 9

Be Positive

It was a warm summer day, and I looked out the second-floor window at the green fields surrounding the Review and Herald offices at Hagerstown. I noticed a lost bee vainly trying to get to the bouquet of flowers on the window ledge inside. I wondered if I'd have any more luck getting into print than the bee was having getting into the room.

Anxious, hopeful, and excited, I sat in the chair opposite Ginger Church, managing editor of *Celebration!* I wanted to share my writing with others but didn't know how to get into print.

Ginger's enthusiasm for her job and people is infectious, and she demonstrated her faith in me by giving me the first writing assignment I had ever received.

She asked me to write "Suddenly I'm Alone" with the passion I'd displayed while talking to her, but with a difference.

"You must write positively," she stressed. "I can't use anything negative in *Celebration!*" After the half-hour interview with Ginger, which ended with prayer, I felt more positive than I had for a long time. God probably couldn't use my negativism any more than Ginger could.

The day I sat in Ginger's office during the second Writers' Week at the Review I was ready to take off my "poor me" and "martyr" garments. Others had suggested I move from my self-absorption but were not in a position to offer me the motivation I needed to change my "poor me" attitude.

Now it was time to consciously change my outlook on life. I might not suddenly become a happy, joyful person again, but I resolved to give the positive more space in my life.

About this time Bobby gave me the book *Living Alone and Liking It.* I wondered how I could possibly live alone and like it. I was struggling with the mechanics of living alone, and hadn't thought in terms of liking it. "Coping," "enduring," or "hanging on" better described my process.

However, the time had come to act "as if" I was feeling positive even when I wasn't. I needed to see beyond my present problems to future possibilities. I needed to look on life as a cup half full instead of a cup half empty. Instead of awakening "to another day without Bob," I could say, " 'This is the day which the Lord hath made;' I will 'rejoice and be glad in it' [Ps. 118:24]."

Art Linkletter's message to anyone who is confronted with the task of picking up the pieces and putting them back together after a devastating tragedy is simple: "Turn scars into stars." His youngest daughter died in a drug-related suicide.

And Carol Schuller, daughter of Dr. Robert Schuller, was in a bad accident. A broken thighbone ruptured the skin, allowing dirt into the wound. To save her, it was necessary to amputate part of her leg. Now Carol tells others, "Look at what you have left, not at what you have lost." She is glad she still has her thigh and knee.

Finally I was ready to start "dealing creatively with the

harsh facts of human existence and still keep on believing in good outcomes." I was on my way to becoming the tough-minded optimist Norman Vincent Peale writes about.

I had been a contented person before Bob's death, and decided I could become more like the person he had fallen in love with in the first place. To do this meant looking on the crises in my life as challenges. Though challenges are not always crises, a crisis is always a challenge and provides an opportunity for growth not possible otherwise. It was up to me to find the opportunity, grasp it, and move with it. Peale wrote that "any soul-wrenching experience carries with it the opportunity for growth." My soul had been wrenched.

Sometimes renaming something will change it from negative to positive. I can label time alone as "loneliness" or "solitude." I can label the suggestions of others as "bossiness" or "caring." I can call people "two-faced" or "tactful."

What positive could I find in hearing loss? A participant in a workshop once asked me, "What are you going to do with the gift of deafness?" "Gift" is such a positive word—it seemed like an odd one to use in labeling something as negative as I was feeling toward my hearing loss. The ultimate was to rename something I'd considered a curse a "gift."

To that point I had seen approaching deafness as nothing but a symbol of old age and didn't want to be reminded that I am growing old. Could I change my perception of hearing loss as a symbol of aging to that of a gift?

Then I remembered visiting a friend who has acute hearing. When I went to bed, she apologized for the loud ticking of the clock in her guest room. "Don't worry," I assured her. "Once my hearing aids are out, I don't hear anything farther than a couple inches from my ear."

Her answer, "You're lucky," made me angry at the time. How could she say I was lucky when I was losing my hearing? I hadn't thought of the sleep she'd lost because she was so aware of every little sound during the night. I could count freedom from disturbance when I want to sleep as a gift.

It is also a gift when unknown voices on the phone ask me to donate or subscribe. Now I simply say "I have a hearing loss and I'm not hearing all you say" and hang up. (I don't hear all anybody says on the phone even with an amplified telephone handset and a t-switch on my hearing aid.)

I am resolved to consciously, constantly, and consistently change my negative attitude toward hearing loss. I need to mourn the loss of advantages to good hearing and let go of the feeling that I have a right to hear well for my whole life, all the while holding on to God's many promises.

In *The Power of Positive Thinking*, written by Norman Vincent Peale, I found a rich resource of ideas for conquering negative thought patterns. As I read the experience of others, I realized I had been struggling, and sometimes whining, with resentment because of problems I was facing. I mistrusted my ability to meet my new responsibilities and had a hard time seeing opportunities, let alone grasping them. I did not possess the "triumphant thought pattern" Peale refers to. What I needed was a vacuum cleaner to suck out my negative attitudes.

I decided that whenever a negative thought came to my mind, I would replace it with a positive one. The thought that I could never keep up our home by myself was recurrent. I could cancel out that negative with "I can do all things through Christ who strengtheneth me" (Phil. 4:13).

And I could reassure myself that I was doing a "good enough" job. My standards for keeping up the yard didn't have to be the same as Bob's. And the inside of the house needs to be clean enough only to be healthy. Accumulation of dust on furniture doesn't have to become a source of unhappiness.

I discovered the truth of Peale's statement that "control with God establishes within us a flow of the same type of energy that re-creates the world and that renews spring every year." And Isaiah promises that "they that wait upon the Lord shall renew their strength; they shall mount up with wings as eagles; they shall run, and not be weary; and they shall walk, and not faint" (Isa. 40:31).

I tried emptying my mind of insecurity, fear, guilt, and regret, and filling it with peaceful experiences. I used positive, restful words as "calm," "secure," and "tranquil."

Finally I realized that I could, with God's help, consciously make the choice to be happy every morning when I awakened. I could run a mental slide show of the happy experiences I expected that day. I already knew there were golden moments in every day, but I had allowed negative attitudes to hide them.

As I write, I'm flat on my back because of a wrenched muscle. I can say either "O Lord, how could You?" or "Lord, is this the way my prayer 'Slow me down' is being answered?" The choice is mine.

A negative thought pattern is inhibiting. It can cause ballplayers to freeze their muscles and throw their timing off so that there is no free flow of power through the team. The story is told of a ball team in the Southwest that was consistently losing. Finally someone had the idea of blessing their bats, and subsequently they worked their way up to a league championship.

Now, if a man blessing bats could have such a powerful effect because the team believed, how much more can our belief in Christ do for us. William James pointed out that the greatest factor in any undertaking is one's belief in it.

Thoreau told us that the secret of achievement is to hold a picture of a successful outcome in mind.

The following statements can be written or typed on

cards and placed in strategic places around the house if remaining positive is a problem. You probably have favorites of your own.

Plato: "Take charge of your life. You can do what you will with it."

Marcus Aurelius: "The soul is dyed the color of its thoughts."

Emerson: "You can if you think you can. A man is what he thinks about all day long."

Dickens (adapted): "We wear the chains we forge in life."

Luke 17:21: "The kingdom of God is within you."

Romans 6:4: "We also should walk in newness of life."

Joshua 1:9: "For the Lord thy God is with thee whithersoever thou goest."

Constant exposure to these statements supports a positive attitude. One day I wrote in my journal, "I really am not lonely much—maybe because I've written it out of my script."

I can think my way to failure and unhappiness, but I can also think my way to success and happiness. The world I live in is determined primarily by the thoughts that habitually occupy my mind, and not by outward conditions and circumstances.

Positive self-talk can help us perceive the world positively.

1. "How thankful and fortunate I am to have four children who care" versus "My life is empty without Bob."

2. "I'm so glad I have a good car and legs so I can get around" versus "I'm tired of going and coming alone."

3. "I feel lucky there are so many things I enjoy doing that don't require hearing" versus "It's a real downer living alone with poor hearing."

Let the life . . . have an absorbing purpose.
—Ellen G. White

Chapter 10

FINDING A PURPOSE

I was sitting in my favorite reading spot—bed. An old corduroy bolster supported my back and a down quilt covered me. A delicate pink was pushing the blackness of the night from the lake and a comparable process was happening within me. After a night of sorrow I could see the promise of a new day.

Twice I read, "Each of us wants to feel that we are not just another grain of sand lying on the beach called humanity . . . that each of us is here to contribute to life on earth something no one else can contribute in quite the same way. At its very minimum, then, your search for a sense of mission arises out of the wish that the world be at least a little bit richer for your being here, and a little bit poorer after your going" (National Career Development Project of United Ministries in Education, No. 2, 1987).

I knew the world was richer for Bob's life and poorer after his death. And that his death was made easier because of the purpose and meaning of his life. Would the same be said for me when I died? It could only if I found a purpose and then fit each activity into my overall purpose.

I picked up my journal, not to write but to read. I was looking for a thread of purpose. I found that after the cancer had spread, I had written, "My purpose is to do all I can to help Bob recuperate. . . . Without him I don't know what the purpose of my life will be."

About the same time I had written, "I want to share the beauty and tranquillity of this place with everybody I know." I knew I could do that without Bob.

But after Bob's death I didn't have the energy or desire to keep going, let alone reach out. I felt "diminished, cut down, incomplete."

"I don't want to eat. I don't want to get dressed. I just want to curl up into a ball and cry and cry. . . . I am not a whole person anymore." Before I could share with others, I needed to pick up the shattered pieces of my life.

At first I was barely able to do what was necessary. "Life seems so meaningless and empty. . . . The thought that my life is without meaning is like quicksand. . . . I have made some attempts to find meaning for my life. . . . I'm not doing enough to justify my existence. . . . I'm too self-centered. . . . Will I ever have enough energy to do more than just care for me? . . . I will be able to get involved in life again when the right opportunity comes along."

Obviously I had expected opportunity to knock on my door, instead of going out and finding opportunities. But I was striving for personal growth and depth. I had believed for years that God would be responsible for the breadth of my life, but that I was responsible for the depth.

At that stage the goals had been small. "Keeping a fire going—symbolic of the warmth I want to feel for life—has become very important to me. And that is so hard to hang on to right now."

Some goals had been written in the negative. "I don't want to be one of the eight out of ten who become ill or injured following a significant loss."

However, there was the pull toward the future: "Do I have the courage and strength to turn the tragedy of Bob's death into a triumph?" It was a difficult task, and I was "unable, uninterested, and even unwilling to go on."

But I had written, "The winter of my mourning is allowing me insights into myself that are covered during sunny times." And because understanding myself better had been a goal for a long time, I'd realized I hadn't lost sight of my purpose completely. "I must make another high point that I can look back on and say 'I grew here.' "

"Pulling together future plans that will make me feel fulfilled, I think of the bridges I am building to the future. Sometimes they seem so fragile—not strong enough to hold the weight of my life." Sometimes I forget that I don't have to build a bridge strong enough to hold the weight of my life alone. God is always beside me.

Later: "I am trying to regain the feeling of being in charge [of my life]. . . . I do have control over how I react to widowhood. . . . I am doing things I have chosen to do, activities that are meaningful to me." There were many worthy causes I could have volunteered for if I had been looking for busywork.

"God, You know I want to bless others, but I will choose the avenue myself rather than having someone else arbitrarily thrust it onto me. I do want to feel fulfilled and will do so only if I choose my own mission in life—not have it put on me as an ill-fitting garment belonging to another."

It was very important to me that I occupy myself by doing things in line with my purpose in life—not what another thought my purpose should be.

I started to do not only what was necessary but also some things that were possible, like the "redefining and restructuring of old relationships." Doing some "things we'd planned on doing together—alone." And "I have achieved my purpose in writing [Memories]. It helped me work through a difficult issue."

Back when I was "trying to justify my existence" and doing barely what was necessary, I had written, "I want to do some education of people relative to handling loss."

Now I find myself doing what seemed impossible then.

Many have searched for meaning and purpose in life. After much struggle I decided that sharing insights regarding my personal loss experience would give meaning to my life. And so I needed to spend time focusing on my goals. I wanted to be sure my short-term goals supported my purpose in life. For example, one way to share the insights I had was through writing, only I wasn't sure I could write anything anybody would want to read.

So taking a writing class became a short-term goal. Besides learning more about writing, I gained new friends who helped balance the time I spent alone. Another short-term goal was to learn word processing. I bought a computer and practiced.

In goal setting it is important to clarify your desires, wants, and dreams. Satisfaction will come when you determine what you want and then see that it happens.

Notice what you don't have that you want and what you have that you don't want. Dissatisfaction is usually a necessary ingredient for change. We function best when striving for something we lack.

There is danger in staying comfortable. We need to move beyond the familiar and deal with the resistance we have to new things. Sometimes we are thrown out of the familiar and have no choice but to make a change. What change we make is up to us.

One couple in Illinois decided that their life lacked meaning. They sold a beautiful four-bedroom home 40 miles from Chicago and now live in two small rooms at a shelter for the homeless where they volunteer full-time.

In making goals, I sort through my needs and beliefs, I challenge existing structures, and set priorities. All the while I must be aware of the negative and positive feelings that arise as I deal with change.

I want my goals to be adjustable, attainable, and maintainable. In order to succeed, I need to stay excited about them. Writing down what I want and when I want it is helpful. And writing it down in positive language, as if it has already been attained, is even more helpful.

Shortly after I got the computer, I wrote, "I can operate my computer with no anxiety." That was wishful thinking then, but true now. It was an atttainable goal that I can maintain.

Last year I wrote, "I have a hearing dog." That was not true then or now, but I was flexible enough to put that goal on hold when I realized I didn't want to be tied down right now. I installed flashing lights that alert me to sounds.

I need to consider past goals. How are they fitting into the purpose for my life? I want to add new goals. My newest one is to learn sign language. It is in line with my overall purpose to communicate with people. The dis-ease I feel in trying to understand words tumbling from hands instead of mouths is considerable. I wonder if I'll ever be comfortable.

My friend Judy is hearing, but noticed deaf people were often isolated. She chose to learn sign language as the purpose to give meaning to her life. Now she is getting arthritis in her hands and may need to be adaptable and change to a different goal. Her vision is now of Christ at the roadside saying "I want you to turn here." Maybe it's just a detour. Maybe she's being completely rerouted. But she's adjusting.

In some areas we cannot be flexible. The three Hebrews were inflexible. God walked with them in the fiery furnace, and they came out unharmed. Many in more recent times walked into the gas chambers of concentration camps with the Lord's Prayer on their lips. The way they approached death gave meaning to their lives. God was with them, too, though they did not walk out.

The same God is with you as you plan goals that are in line with your purpose, which will then give meaning to your life.

"Our souls are hungry for meaning, for the sense that we have figured out how to live so that our lives matter. . . . What frustrates us and robs our lives of joy is this absence of meaning."—Harold Kushner.

Pain, loss, and death are all easier if there is a purpose and meaning to life.

These things have I spoken unto you, . . . that your joy might be full.

—John 15:11

Chapter 11

Joyful Again

It was another year and another crisp spring morning in New England. Cotton candy clouds sailed above, leafing trees promised summer shade, and balloons decorated the lobby of the New England Memorial Hospital. April 10, 1988, dedication day of the G. Robert Rigsby Maternity Center, had arrived. Shortly before his death the hospital administrator and good friend, Wolfgang von Maack, told Bob this unit would be named in his honor. And now Bob's dream had become a reality.

Dressed in an off-white suit I'd spent more time finding than I had my wedding dress, I stood in the conference room waiting for the keynote speaker, Dr. Benjamin Spock. A friend approached me with tears in his eyes. "This day is empty without Bob," he said.

"Yes," I responded, "but today is a day of celebration."

While cooperating with the Public Relations Department of the hospital in their preparation for the dedication, I decided I needed the day to be one of joyous celebration of Bob's life. Since the funeral the children had not all been home at the same time. I wanted the experience of closeness we had then without the deep sadness.

I thought of the funeral as one of a pair of bookends and the dedication as the other. In between was (1) *Allowing Grief,* (2) *Strategies for Coping With Loss*, (3) *Focus on the Positive*, (4) *Finding a Purpose*, and finally (5) *Joyful Again.* I felt progression as far as the contents of the first four volumes, but joy seemed locked in a room I couldn't reach.

Then I found that joy and suffering could coexist. Life could be joyful and satisfying without Bob in person. The sadness of missing Bob could be eclipsed by the joy of living.

I knew that joy was a by-product rather than an end in itself. If I search for joy and happiness, it can be illusive. If I search for service, the joy will come. I must be aware of opportunities and rays of light.

Years ago I read a story titled "Joy Cometh in the Morning." A young girl's fiancé was killed in an automobile accident on his way to the church where they were to be married. She clung to God's promises that He would come again and wipe all tears from our eyes. She and her fiancé would then be reunited, and she could be joyful again.

But what of the years between a loss and eventual reunion with our loved ones? Will they be tainted or tinted by the loss? The loss will change our lives in one way or another. A loss can cause persons to close in on themselves so tightly that no shaft of the light of joy can penetrate their gloom; or it can be a stepping-stone.

I can remember unwillingly visualizing myself in a black pit into which no shaft of light could penetrate. It was so pitch-dark that I could see nothing and had to rely on my sense of touch.

Then one day while I was meditating it seemed as if a door had been opened ever so slightly and a shaft of light entered the darkness. Had it been there all along and I hadn't noticed it? I knew I could choose to live in the continual darkness of my sorrow or start living so that joy was the by-product.

Staying in the darkness was out of the question—we are made to be joyful, happy people. Expecting others to supply the joy in my life was unreasonable and often meant disappointment. I started looking for joy in its many disguises.

I looked at the people I enjoyed being with and realized they were independent and busy and didn't need me to complete themselves. Well, I would try to become the same.

I realized I had been like the missing piece in Shel Silverstein's *Big O*. I had been looking for someone outside of myself to complete me. I needed to be able to roll along by myself or in company with another, but not as part of another.

Recently I wrote in my journal, "I do not need anyone to complete me. Complement and compliment, but not complete." Another goal reached. I am not very joyful when I sit and wait for others to share their joy with me. I need a reliable source within me.

Telling myself that I could be a source of joy/light instead of expecting others to be my supply was a beginning. I decided to generate happiness instead of gloom. And I learned to be more patient with myself. I could allow my joy/light to go out without despairing about relighting it. I could handle periods of darkness without feeling deprived or picked upon. It was as if I needed to make periodic trips into the darkness to appreciate the light. If I felt sad on an anniversary, I could allow myself to cry awhile and then go about my work for the day. In other words, I was gaining control of my life.

On the road to becoming joyful, I started consciously recording the positive, creative, and life enhancing experiences in my journal. Recording happiness makes it doubly rewarding because I can read what I've written. I support and give power to whatever I focus on in my writing. This balances my painful and joyful perceptions. I tried throwing away writings about discouraging experiences.

Every day I have chances to decide to be joyful and act accordingly. Today I can choose to give in to self-pity because I have a bad headache and Blue Cross premiums have just been raised. Or I can choose to be glad I found comfortable walking shoes while shopping and that my ear infection is clearing up.

I can enjoy the now of spending time with grandchildren on the West Coast, or I can dwell on how bad I feel because the coasts are far apart. Every morning I can open a package labeled "joyous certainty."

Sometimes joy is a quiet thing; at other times it can be explosive. It may represent the total coming together of all parts, giving a feeling of completeness. Sometimes it is like a gift, or a surprise that comes out of the blue. If I can trust God more fully and believe in myself, I will find more joy in the everyday of my life. There is joy in doing the right thing at the right time.

Sorrow and joy can exist together in the same person.

The deeper sorrow cuts into me, the more joy I can hold.

It takes a decision and commitment to focus on the joy in life.

Each transition is an ending that prepares the ground for new growth and new activities.

—William Bridges

Chapter 12

THE BEGINNING

Transitions are composed of endings, neutral zones, and beginnings. Sometimes a new life is built on a satisfied dream, sometimes on a shattered dream. Very often endings are the result of something gone wrong. We have no choice in a death, a job layoff, the burning of a beloved home. They can be terrifying happenings as they break the connection with the setting in which we are familiar.

But most endings and losses do not represent finality. They involve symbolic deaths; you let go of the old and pick up the new. Endings can be doorways to new activities and achievements. But building a new life means taking unknown and sometimes frightening routes. It involves acting in unfamiliar ways, but eventually means living again.

Graduations and most immigrations are endings that have been chosen. They are transitions that can be key times in the natural process of self-renewal. Yet there is a neutral zone time during which one is part of neither the old nor the new.

It is important to stay in this zone long enough to make

the right beginning. Take time to dream, for dreams can guide your choices and give direction to your life. If they are for the good of yourself and others, they are God's invitation to spread your wings and fly to new heights.

But the emptiness of this neutral space can be overwhelming, especially if you have few continuities during the time. As the loss of a loved person begins a process of mourning, so does a move from one's homeland. Immigrants who have no friends or relatives nearby might suffer a lot from lack of continuity.

Lack of continuity was a big factor in the difficulty I had in adjusting to widowhood. But I did take the time to discover what I really wanted. I stayed in the neutral zone long enough to know what a right beginning might be for me.

Because I believe that genuine beginnings depend on inner reorganization rather than external shifts, I have been alert to the inner signals that cue me into the nearness of new beginnings.

I didn't recognize the seed of a new beginning when a friend asked recently, "Have you thought of networking among the deaf and hard-of-hearing?"

But the seed thought was planted, and shortly afterward, during an extended visit with my children in California, I decided to take sign language. My daughter found a tutor willing to teach us all—Kaiti, 5; Meg, 7; Shirley; and me. Shirley's enthusiasm was infectious. But after the first few lessons my reaction was "What a poverty-stricken way to communicate. There are so few words compared to English."

Then I saw a well-known hymn signed in church, and realized that there was a dimension to American Sign Language I had never understood before. The language is rich in emotion. It's not inferior—only different.

I returned to Massachusetts knowing how important it was for me to take a class in sign language and find a community who signed. As a first step I went to the Learning Center for the Deaf in Framingham. It felt wonderful to be with people who accepted poor hearing as normal.

While touring the children's school, I suddenly saw how some pieces of my life's puzzle could fit. Here was where I might best be able to use my scholastic background in early childhood education and in counseling as well as the practical experience of raising four children.

I thought to myself, *Maybe this is* the *new beginning I've been waiting for—if not, there will be another if I keep in touch with the small voice within me.*

By the end of 1989 I'd made a solid beginning in writing and teaching, but I was practically illiterate as far as reading hands. So I added that problem to my list. One of my students was honest enough to tell me that I complain too much. I laughed and said, "Aren't you glad I've turned in your grade already?"

"It wouldn't have made any difference, I'm sure," he answered.

It was near the end of my third year of widowhood that I felt an echo within me when I read in *Starting Over* that bereavement specialists now realize it takes at least three years to complete the process of grieving. "Most people find they have to work hard at feeling better for the first two years following the death. By the third year, you don't have to work so hard, you feel better all by yourself, even though you have temporary setbacks."

Nineteen ninety would be a new year and a new decade. I determined to make it a new era. I needed to do something different over which I had control. Circumstances had forced me from my role of sheltered wife to anguished widow. But I realized that was a transition period. It was time to choose to be an independent woman.

What changes could I make so I would feel more in control? I had waited long past the year most advise before making a major change. I could sell my house and move. But that was the path of no return, and I might be sorry.

Then one evening I went to the medicine cabinet to get headache medication for the fourth time in one day. I realized that my headaches were controlling me. That was something I could control, and if I did, I wouldn't feel like a fake teaching a class on stress and illness while I coped with my stresses through medication.

About that time a friend who had headaches stopped all medication "cold turkey." I wondered if I was strong enough to do that. I remembered Philippians 4:13, "I can do all things through Christ which strengtheneth me." It was possible, but I knew myself well enough to know I'd need human support to kick a habit that began 25 years ago. A habit of popping a pill for pain instead of changing my lifestyle.

Where would I find the human support I needed? I prayed, phoned, and wrote letters.

In the end I went to a reconditioning center in Norway. I had many reasons for choosing to go there. My father was Norwegian; crossing the Atlantic had often meant big changes in my life; and the answer to my query letter was extremely cordial.

The supportive environment there included old friends, the Hogganviks, from Ethiopia days, and the dedicated workers at Fredheim, who became new friends. They were all so caring and hopeful that I knew I would never become a health center dropout. I had come too far and had too much at stake. The new decade might not be headache-free, but I would not use drugs in place of a change in lifestyle.

Eating the right foods, drinking more water, exercising regularly, and massage all helped to lessen my headaches as well as my weight and cholesterol level.

My grandparents left the shores of Norway more than

100 years ago to begin a new life in America. I left America bound for Norway and my new beginning.

While cherishing many precious memories, I am now ready to reinvest myself in life without Bob. I am ready to say goodbye to my old life and hello to whatever the new has to offer.

The other day as I drove I found myself singing the last verse of *Prayer Perfect*. "Do I really mean all the words?" I asked myself. And I could truthfully answer, "Yes."

> "Give unto the sorrowing all release from pain.
> Let the lips of laughter overflow again.
> And to all the weary, O divide I pray
> This vast treasure of content that is mine today."

It is for our own benefit to keep every gift of God fresh in our memory.

—Ellen G. White

Chapter 13

MEMORIES

We have lived so long together . . . ; we have been so close that nothing can separate us now: surely nothing so inconclusive as death. Do you imagine that merely by leaving my side your father leaves me alone? How can I ever be alone? . . . Memories are stronger than the living flesh. Your father has died, but not in me; as long as I remain on this earth he will never die" (Irving Stone, *Immortal Wife*, p. 449).

I read the paragraph over and over. I wrote the words over and over as if on bark, where they would deepen as time lengthened. Was this what my therapist meant when she said "Memory nourishes the heart and grief abates. Gain nurturance from your memories"?

One of the earliest definitions of *memory* is "a service for the dead." Today it is defined as a "process for remembering." For some the gradual diminishing of memory is necessary before they can relinquish the past. For others memory is a means of preserving the presence of the dead. Too often the presence is preserved along with an overpowering sense of loss. I believe it is possible to preserve the presence of the dead without a constant, aching, longing pain that so often comes with a sense of presence. "He lives within my heart" can become a joyful reality relative to a person as well as to Christ in the heart. This will not happen if memory is allowed to take over without any guidance from me.

How can I best go about the task of organizing my memories so they will be readily available to me when I need them? Leaving them in disarray is as discouraging to me as a trip to the attic. I moved practically everything from our Boston home 10 weeks before Bob died. I didn't have time to sort. Everything in the attic is symbolic of some memory, and I've not had the energy to sort symbols or memories. I don't want everything, and am tired of stumbling across material things or mental images I could be getting rid of.

Friday I cleared the entryway to the attic. Today I will start with my memories. So many around the house bring sadness. It was here that the cancer metastasis became evident and Bob's symptoms multiplied. He had no appetite, he stumbled, he hurt. Bob lived those days once. I've lived them a thousand times. But there is pure gold to be panned from those sad days. I want to carry the gold into the future and leave the dross behind. We faced mortality together and learned that we were strong enough to face the future as long as we remembered who held it, and didn't borrow worry and anxiety from it. We learned to live one day, and sometimes one hour, at a time.

I can see from my dining room window across the lake to the first house we considered buying in early 1986 when Bob was thinking in terms of retiring. The house was too small and too expensive, but the first tangible picture of a dream. We talked about remodeling if the price became affordable. We tried the dream on for size, as it were. The next house was too far from the road, with a large yard to keep up. But the more we looked, the more we knew our retirement dream of living on the lake was the right dream to pursue to reality.

The day after Bob's surgery I saw this house. It was love at first sight. The joy of the find and the work of the move propelled me through August and September. I want to tap into the faith, hope, and joy of those busy days. I need the strength they can give. We had searched together, we moved together. I'm determined not to let my sadness at being left overshadow the joy that was. I choose not to focus on the dark days.

And then I look around the house we shared for so short a time. I could go into each room and write a chapter on the happy memories brought to mind by the furniture, pictures, and other accessories. I remember the excitement of going to our first flea market as I write at the large antique oak desk we bought. It was a bargain and a compromise, for I'd wanted a rolltop. But a rolltop would have blocked my view of the lake.

I relive the happy hours of our Scotland adventure when I look at the dishes displayed in the glass-doored corner cabinet on the right. I can see Bob carefully checking each hand-painted dish we bought from the factory in Crieff. They were thirds that he insisted were better than some of the seconds when carefully chosen. The left cabinet triggers different happy memories. We both enjoyed camping and antique hunting with complete abandon and stopped at every flea market and antique shop up and down the coast of New England in search of ruby-red glassware. Each piece has a story, where it came from and how we got it.

Sharing increases the nurturance value of memories. Last month was pregnant with opportunities. I spent time with my brother and his family, Brenda from mission field days, and Dessa from medical school days. She did not take the advice of a well-meaning person who suggested, "And you know not to talk to Joyce about Bob." Of course we talked about Bob. Because I cry sometimes does not mean that I do not want to talk about him. My bond to those with whom I can share the memory of Bob's life and death is strong.

The children and grandchildren are my richest source of memories—and surest point of pain. Happenings today trigger memories that only Bob could fully share. Learning to accept the sometime pain of memory is where my growth lies.

Of course I'm not naive enough to think I can be in total control of my memories. A sniff of perfume, a snatch of melody, a shaft of moonlight are all capable of evoking memories that bring pain or pleasure. Whether my memories burn or bless, hurt or heal, is to some extent in my control. When the Bible promises, "Blessed are they that mourn," I'm sure the author doesn't intend that I tap into a painful vein every time I have a memory of Bob. But it is within my control to make every past memory painful as long as I link it with the thought that Bob should be here now. If instead of counting the years I had with him I count the years without him, the pain of my loss will be perpetuated.

My struggle to write this chapter on memories is symbolic of my struggle to reach and hold on to the many happy memories of my life with Bob. It is so much easier to reach and hold on to the memories that bring me pain and sadness. They crowd around the doors of my mind and heart, knocking insistently and not waiting to be invited inside. They jostle for space and chatter constantly.

I know that I must acknowledge and allow all memories, but I can put limits on the least-productive ones. I don't have to run a continuous slide show of Bob's last days. By dwelling on Bob's death, am I allowing it to have a greater impact on me than his life? I'm working on putting my memories into proper perspective. I want to start a journal titled "Happy Memories." I'll write the unhappy ones down on scrap paper and throw them away.

I'm resolved to avoid guilt trips as I journey down memory's paths. I did the best I could at the time. Now it's easy to see what I might have done differently, but playing "if only" tapes over and over won't be nearly as nurturing as playing "I accept what was."

It is important as I move into single living that I start a new set of memories. Today a friend came over and said, "Every Easter Sunday we'll get together. It will be a tradition." I need to establish many traditions to build a satisfying life.

This summer I invited foreign students over for potlucks.

In the fall I can plan to take someone who has no car to see the foliage.

As I live in relation to others, it will be hard to add to my store of memories without adding to theirs, and hard to add to theirs without adding to my own.

I will learn to make more happy memories. Memories that will heal and bless me and those whose lives I touch.

Empty

Your chair—
It's empty.
I saw it through tears
As I awakened
Wishing
You were here.

The bed—
Empty too,
Except for grief
And me.
Shared intimacies
Felt, spoken, heard—
Forever only memory.

Your role—
Is empty.
Vacant, void,
AWOL.
Husband,
Friend, and lover
Irrevocably gone.

My heart—
Empty
Though leaden.
Nobody ever told me
Emptiness
Was a load
So heavy to carry.

The tomb—
It's empty!
Joyful thought.
All my needs can be filled
When
He enters.

—Joyce Rigsby